IMAGINE DRAGONS

THE PROJECT 2.0

by

Ingrid Müller &

Constantinos Poluchronopoulos

Cover Illustration Copyright © 2022 by Anastasia Blinkova and Constantinos Poluchronopoulos
Cover design by Anastasia Blinkova and Constantinos Poluchronopoulos
Design and production by Ingrid Müller and Constantinos Poluchronopoulos
Editing by Ingrid Müller, Lou & Don Wilkinson & Celeste Horrocks
Chapter opening and general illustrations © 2022 Anastasia Blinkova
Poems used in this book: I Found A Band, Gold Guitar, Wonderful, Peculiar Bassist, Music & Monsters Copyright © 2022 Rachel Isabella Fealy

QR codes created with QR-Generator (free version) https://www.the-qrcode-generator.com

We´ve created this book with love and dedicate it to

IMAGINE DRAGONS

and to all the Firebreathers out there...

Ingrid   Anastasia   Celeste   Rachel

Imagine Dragons
@Imaginedragons

amazing job with this book and
thanks to everyone supporting
@TRFdotORG

Twitter, December 29, 2020

So... here we are. I can't believe that this project, which Ingrid and I have been working on for the past few months, has finally been released! It's something that we wanted to do, for all of you... this is a gift, from the fans, to the fans. Made with lots of love, and endless passion that we have for our Dragons.
I couldn't be more proud of this work. I hope you'll have a great time reading this book. This is yours. Welcome on board!

Constantinos (Ken)

Why do we love Imagine Dragons? Well, there are a million reasons, but don't worry, I won't mention them all. Everyone is different, everyone makes different decisions, has different attitudes, different beliefs; well, there are so many different things that can divide us, but only one that unites us.... Our admiration, passion, and our love for this band.
It's so much more than just four guys, creating music.
It's an attitude towards life.
This book celebrates these four very special humans, with some fun, some information, some a-ha moments, and maybe there are a few things that you didn't known about Imagine Dragons.
Let's find out!

Ingrid (maya0811)

But first, we'd like to say a heartfelt THANK YOU and give all our love to:

Anastasia (Nastya): You're one of the most talented people we know. This project wouldn't be the same without you. It was such an honor working with you. We love you!

To the Firebreathers on Twitter and Facebook: Thank you to everyone who participated in this project. We love you all, every single one of you. You're all such unique human beings. **Georgia**, my beloved firebreather.. love you a lot.

Penny: You're a very close friend of mine, and such a special person. I love you, thank you for always being there for me.

TRF: Our motivation to bring this book to life, thank you for trusting us to release this project. And **Kim Gradisher:** Thank you for providing this awesome interview!

LoveLoud (Clarissa Savage): We appreciate your time and efforts to provide an outstanding Interview and giving us a small insight to this awesome organization. Thank you!

KultureCity (Daniel Platzman): Thank you for taking the time to answer our question about KultureCity and for your help to shed a light on this amazing charity organization!

Lou & Don: This book would not be possible without your help! Thank you for helping us finalize this book.

Ingrid M.: My soulmate, best friend, and strongest critic.... You're one of a kind! Thank you so much for your opinion, and for putting up with my moods, it's very much appreciated. Sending you big hugs.

Wolfgang: Thank you for your love, support, patience and for building me up when I had doubts about this project, and myself. I love you to the Moon and back.

Rachel: Your poems are incredible and we´re so thankful and honored that you´ve provided them for this book.

Celeste: Thank you for jumping in and for all your passion and love for this project! You are amazing and we love you!

Constantinos (mercurialkenny): Thank you from the bottom of my heart for being the best co-author ever! Your passion, your love & belief for this project is just incredible. You will always have a special place in my heart... my bff!   Ingrid

Ingrid (maya0811): My partner, I love you with my whole heart. Thank you so much for making me your partner in this incredible project. You're very special to me, and I'm so grateful that we had the opportunity to work together.   Kenny

Matt Eastin: We really appreciate your support and help with our project. We are so grateful that you´ve invested a great amount of your time to improve our article about you... and also for telling us a few secrets...

Tim and Amy Cantor: Mr. Cantor provided the artwork for the album Smoke + Mirrors and he was so kind to have a closer look at our article about him and to approve it. Thank you so much for your time and effort. We feel so honored!

amyums#4858, Didicelis21#7519, Meghamnsingh#7643, Ethan-jalapeno#7474, Hippiecat#9751 and Adayinthelifeof#1530 from Discord: Thank you for your help and support for our project! !

Jesse Robinson: It was a pleasure and an honor to speak to you about your brother Tyler. Thank you for your time!

Mac Reynolds: Thank you so much for taking the time to read through our project and for all your help and support leading to its release.

Daniel Coulter Reynolds, Daniel Wayne Sermon, Benjamin Arthur McKee, Daniel James Platzman: You're not just a band. Imagine Dragons are an ideal, a feeling of hope, a desire for more, a celebration of life. You make this world a better place with your music. This book is about you, but it´s also for you. You have changed our lives, our attitude towards life and love, you´ve taught us to be grateful.

With your help, we've learned to live in the here and now, to accept and celebrate our feelings, our strengths, and also our weaknesses. Thank you for reading and supporting our project! You mean the world to us. We love you!

Let´s find out how well you know the band.....

Question 1:
Is it true that the band had a different name for a short time?

O Yes
O No

Question 2:
Which member of Imagine Dragons broke his hand during a performance?

O Dan
O Wayne
O Ben
O Platz
O None of them

Question 3:
Who has a monkey phobia?

O Dan
O Wayne
O Ben
O Platz
O None of them

Question 4:
Have Imagine Dragons ever won a Grammy award?

○ Yes
○ No

Question 5:
Which member was the last one to join the band?

○ Wayne
○ Ben
○ Platz

Question 6:
Two band members have similar tattoos....Who are they?

○ Wayne and Ben
○ Ben and Platz
○ Dan and Platz

Question 7:
Is it true that Imagine Dragons filmed a fake boxing match with Vladimir Klitschko for one of their music videos?

○ Yes
○ No

I Found A Band

Hey
So, I found this band
No, you'll like them, I promise
Just give them a chance, please?

They're called Imagine Dragons
Yes, I know, just stay with me, okay? Don´t judge
Here, I'll hand you my headphones
Shhh, listen!

Don´t tell me I´m a crazy fangirl
Don´t tell me I just love them for their looks
Please, I´m not like that
(That´s not to say they aren't pretty...)

You want to know why I love them?
Oh boy. I knew this was coming
Hang on a second
This is a heavy one.

This will sound cheesy, so... yeah
I'll try not to make it too poetic
I love them because...
Well, first, because they're freaking awesome.

And sometimes the world feels like it´s crumbling
Sometimes just being alive feels impossible
And all I need to do is plug in my headphones — boom
Instant dopamine, serotonin, all the good stuff.

There are my worried days
The rocking-back-and-forth, fighting tears of terror days
Trapped in the dead of night
Anxiety likes to eat me alive.

And I´m not saying they're magic,
that they make the nasty stuff go away
But when I´m listening to my Dragons, I can breathe again
Because I feel like they're here with me. Here for me
And I can get through this.

See, this is where things get a bit darker
I rarely talk about this part, because -
Because it makes me feel like...
Like that crazy, obsessed fangirl,
Who everyone rolls their eyes at.

But you asked, I'll tell
There are the days I break
Because nothing around me feels real
And I don´t feel real, and I wouldn't deserve it, anyhow

Where I´m crying because I can't take it anymore
Because I feel alone
So alone
And everything is a foggy, shattered disaster.

But they help me pick myself up again
They read my thoughts and put them into songs
That make me cry, but I listen to them anyway
Because they're the family I´ve never met.

And I watch hundreds of their interviews
Because even though they're just a bunch of average guys
Honestly, that´s what I love most
They're not perfect, they're human, and they're here.

And the strength and inspiration they've given me -
I owe them the concert money just in therapy
And I will see them live, even if it takes years to get tickets.
And I will meet them one day. I have to.

So... yeah
I found this band called Imagine Dragons.
They've shown me the flawed, raw beauty in all of us.
And I love them.

Daniel Wayne Sermon

Daniel Wayne Sermon was born on June 15, 1984, in American Fork, Utah. He is one of five children, born to Jeff & Debbie Sermon. He has three older siblings, and one younger sibling. There's a very strong bond between all five of them.

Wayne grew up as a member of The Church of Jesus Christ of Latter-Day Saints. In an interview, he said that he was living his father's dream of performing on stage. His father is also a composer and his mother is a passionate piano player. The family used to make music together, and called themselves "The Sermon Family Band."

Growing up, he loved listening to albums by The Beatles, such as "Abbey Road" and "Rubber Soul". He very much enjoyed the sounds of Tom Scholz (of the band Boston) and particularly liked his approach to solos. Wayne also liked listening to Led Zeppelin and Iron Butterfly. These artists were his introduction to music, and gave him the inspiration to want to learn to play the guitar.

At the age of 8, Wayne started learning to play the piano, and two years later, at age 10, he also learned to play the cello. When he was 12 years old, Wayne visited a music store and fell in love with electric guitars. He got his first electric guitar as a Christmas present, and soon became obsessed with it, practicing for up to 8 hours a day. The first songs he learned to play were by Pearl Jam and Nirvana, as his older brother was a big fan of them.

One day, whilst he and his family were attending a wedding, his father asked a teenaged Wayne, what he was going to do with his life. Wayne was a bit confused, but answered that he may attend law school. His father was baffled and replied that he thought there was something in the stars for him musically. From there on, both parents guided him in the direction of music, and after finishing high school, he went to the Berklee College of Music in Boston.

To gain a scholarship to Berklee, Wayne auditioned in front of a committee, he played a jazz song by Wes Montgomery to showcase his skills.

Wayne was obviously excited to be accepted into Berklee, but after joining, he soon started thinking that he wasn't anything that special. There were hundreds of students like him, and he started to ask himself whether it would have been better to stay in American Fork, as the big fish in a small pond. Thankfully, he stayed at Berklee and decided to buckle down on his studies and work hard.

At Berklee, Wayne met Daniel Platzman and Ben McKee while attending the same classes together, and were also all members of the project "Guitar Lab". Students learned to interact musically, and how to form a band. They formed a jazz fusion ensemble called "The Eclectic Electrics." They even did a few gigs locally around town, but it was mostly just for fun. In 2008, Wayne graduated from Berklee School of Music, with a double major in guitar performance and composition, respectively.

After graduation, Wayne went back to Utah, where he met an old friend from school, who recommended he go see an amazing new musician that he had come across. He thought Wayne would appreciate his music and performance abilities. The musician, in white jeans and a striped T-shirt, was of course - Dan Reynolds. This is how they first met.

Wayne married the love of his life, Alexandra Hall (a ballerina and BYU graduate) on February 18, 2011. The couple first met during Wayne´s last year at Berklee, while he was visiting home for the holidays. They were introduced by Alex´s friend, Brittany. (Who married Andrew Tolman, one of Wayne´s closest friends.) The couple had an immediate connection, even finishing each other's sentences, but stayed as just friends for over a year before beginning to date. As things got more serious between the pair, and after Wayne had joined Imagine Dragons, Alex moved to Las Vegas to be with him. Before their wedding, having only just $500 in his bank account, Wayne sold his guitar to buy wedding rings. At their wedding reception, they danced to the romantic song "Something" by The Beatles. The couple have 3 beautiful children together: River James (July 26, 2014), Wolfgang Alexander (January 21, 2016) and Sunnie Rae (October 5, 2018).

Wayne - Little Known Facts

- He suffers from chronic insomnia, but his songwriting skills benefit from his sleeping problems.

- He occasionally goes by the name Wing Sermon. When their manager introduced them at one of their first shows, it was in a really loud room, and everyone thought he had said "Wing" this nickname stuck with him from then on.

- When asked about his role models, Wayne has said they are Jimi Hendrix, Eric Clapton, and George Harrison, from The Beatles.

- The various guitars and equipment Wayne uses are: Bilt Electric, Gibson Jeff Tweedy SignatureSG, Gibson J-45, Elixir Strings, and Gibson Honky Tonk Deuce.

- He loves the color gold and he mostly uses guitars and equipment in that color on stage..

- He has a monkey phobia, so he wasn't exactly thrilled when his bandmates requested a monkey butler from their management, to see if they would actually get it for them.

- He loves reading, and enjoys playing online games with Dan Reynolds.

- In his opinion, the best album ever is "Rubber soul", by The Beatles.

- Wayne´s Dad, Jeff, witnessed the falling of the Berlin Wall in 1989 when he went back to Germany to visit the place where he served his Mormon mission. He also owns one of the largest collections of Volkswagen and German cars in the US, which he showcases at local auto shows.

- His famous golden guitar is actually made of wood and just covered in gold. Wayne nicknamed it „C3PO".

- Just 3 days after her birth, his daughter, Sunny Rea had to have open heart surgery.

- The first concert Wayne ever attended was to see the band, Third Eye Blind

- He took German lessons at the public high school in American Fork (He was a proud "Caveman" — that's the school mascot).

- Every time Wayne hears an Imagine Dragons song on the radio in his car, he turns down the volume so he can't hear it, instead of turning it off, so it doesn't affect the algorithm on the radio (which decides which songs are played).

- He passed out on stage during the K-pop weenie roast festival in L.A. due to the hot weather. Dan also passed out, and fell into the audience.

- He worked at UPS in customer service, and considers it to be the worst job he's had.

- Wayne and his wife Alex made a five part video podcast about their lives, career and beliefs. If you'd like to watch this, it is on YouTube, please search for "Mormon stories with Wayne and Alex."

- Although he was raised in the Mormon faith, Wayne never attended BYU (Brigham Young University) — a school that is sponsored by the LDS church, and is very popular for Mormons to attend. Instead, he studied at the Berklee College of Music.

- The first guitar solo that Wayne learned to play was from the song "Alive" by Pearl Jam.

- Wayne bought a house in the South Bay area of Los Angeles just days after his friend and bandmate, Dan Reynolds, did the same. It´s located in the rural gated community of Rolling Hills, which has an equestrian logo/crest. The 6 acre ranch, not only has an outside kitchen, stables, a pool and a guesthouse, but also an impressive bonafide observatory.

- Alexandra Hall (Sermon) mentioned in an interview that Wayne is an incredibly talented writer. "I think he should write a book because he's very talented that way," Sermon said. "But he loves guitars so much that I don't know if he sees anything else."

- Wayne has a good sense of fashion. In an interview, he said that corduroy is an absolute NO-GO for him.

- A funny coincidence....We´ve already mentioned how one of Wayne´s nicknames is Wing, well his maternal Grandmother's surname is Wing - Lois Wing!

- Alexandra Sermon (born: Hall) graduated from BYU in 2011 with a degree in journalism and wrote a blog while touring with Imagine Dragons. She documented their daily adventures living on the road in her Blog "From the Dragon Wagon with Love".

- Musical talent runs through Wayne´s blood, his Father, Jeff Sermon, had also released two albums: "Building Bridges To The Heart" and "One Step At A Time" (available on Amazon).

- Dan revealed in an interview that Wayne had a huge crush on Emma Watson.

- The best advice Wayne has ever received is „Don't do music because you want to do music, do music because you have to do music."

- Wayne played hockey in high school!

Gold Guitar

There it sits
Glimmering, glittering glory
Each string echoing memories
Trapped inside the wood

It rests
Plastered with fingerprints and marks
Each one gently carved by life
Sunbeams bouncing off that solid finish

And you didn't know
This would be your image
You didn't know people
Would devour your words, cling to them like a lifeline

That they would beg to get your handwriting
To take a picture with you
Screaming their love, their pride, their joy
Because... you're special?

You never thought you were special
When you lay awake in the dark
Counting the ticking of the clock
Waiting and wishing for something more

You're just an average boy
Turned to an average man
Who did amazing things
Maybe that's why they love you?
Because you are breathing proof
That sometimes it takes an average person
Just like them
To do fantastic things

And you don't really understand it
Even now
Why they're obsessed with you, why they cry
when they see you

But... maybe that's okay
Just keep strumming those strings
Because you have no idea
How much grace you radiate
And how much inspiration you give

You may be average in comparison
But your fans don't see it that way
They see a savior
They see someone who they feel they know, even if
you've never met them

Humans might be the same
All made of the same stuff
That doesn't change the fact
That you created something brilliant

A legacy

You

You and your gold guitar

Daniel James Platzman

Daniel James Platzman was born on September 28, 1986, in Atlanta, Georgia. He has one older brother, and was born into a family of chamber musicians. His parents met while attending college, while performing in musical theatre. His father loved playing piano, so Platz soon followed in his footsteps, and started learning the instrument at the age of 3. A year later he also took up playing the violin.

A few more years passed, and Platz started to learn how to play the drums. Growing up, he listened to a lot of jazz, classical music, and prog-rock. In an interview with DRUM! magazine, he admitted to not being the type of kid that practiced for hours, and even referred to himself as a "cocky music kid".

When he decided he wanted to become a professional musician, his parents were supportive, but they wanted to make sure he had a safety net. Platz didn't want to disappoint his parents, so he chose to do Architectural Acoustics as well, so even his back up plan had something to do with music & sound, which shows just how passionate he is about music. Platz particularly enjoyed going to the Sundance Film Festival; this probably helped influence him to register for a course for film scoring at Berklee College of Music.

After his first year at Berklee, Platz stayed for five weeks on campus during summer break. At the start of the summer break, he thought he was one of the best students there. However, as the fall semester approached, he realized that he still had a huge amount to learn. While at Berklee, he joined the Country Western Ensemble, and also learned African/Cuban drumming because he was so keen to experience something new.

One important technique he was shown, was how to play the drums quietly. This style of drumming was hard for him to get the hang of, as he had used thick hearing protection for years, and therefore was used to playing extremely loudly. Nonetheless, by the end of his time at Berklee, drumming softly became one of his trademarks, which led to him being popular with solo artists, because he could match the variations in volume control so well.

Like Wayne, Platz was also part of the guitar lab group, a project that was taught & overseen by Mark White, which helped guide musicians in how to interact with each other. The group consisted of five guitars, one bass and one drummer. One of the guitar players was of course Wayne Sermon and the bass player? .....That was Platz´s roommate Ben McKee. Platz graduated from Berklee, receiving a Bachelor's Degree in film scoring.

After finishing college, he moved to New York for two and a half years, living out his passion for jazz music. He played a gig at The Elephant Room in New York where it just so happened that Imagine Dragons were also playing there. This led to Platz watching their performance, and then meeting with them. He was blown away by them and made it clear that if the opportunity ever arose, he would love to join the band.

Shortly after, he received a phone call from Ben, saying the band was in need of a drummer. True to his word, Platz packed his bags and immediately moved to Los Angeles where the band was touring in their "Dragon Wagon" between California, Nevada and Utah to perform for their growing fan base. Just a few weeks after their move from Las Vegas to L.A., Imagine Dragons signed a record deal with Interscope Records.

Platz - Little Known Facts

- He attended Paideia High School, a private school located in Druid Hills, Atlanta. He graduated in 2005. While enrolled, he was active on the frisbee team.

- He participated in the prestigious Betty Carter Jazz Ahead program at the Kennedy Center in Washington D.C.

- He received the Vic Firth Award for outstanding musicianship as well as the Michael Rendish award in film scoring.

- Platz says that the moment he knew the band had made it was when Weird Al Yankovic released a parody of "Radioactive"…. He called home and got everyone on the phone to tell them about it, the family went absolutely wild. They freaked out even more about this than when the band were at The Grammys!

- He takes warming up before a live performance very seriously. He needs 45 minutes of warm-up time, and says that every time he hasn't warmed up, he's regretted it.

- When talking to DRUM! magazine, Platz mentioned that he is interested in Heisenbergs theory (quantum mechanics).

- His first job was at an ice cream saloon, during high school. He had to sing a special song every time someone tipped them.

- He is allergic to gluten, so he sticks to a gluten-free diet.

- A lot of lyrics that Platz writes come to him via dreams or nightmares!

- While growing up he went to see trumpeter Russell Gunn, and the drummer Lil´ John Roberts (one of his favorite drummers), he would watch them perform every Thursday. And Lil´ John Roberts style of playing drums very much ended up influencing Platz´s own style.

- He loves playing Mario Kart and loves to sing when he's in the shower.

- His favorite prog-rock band is Gentle Giant.

- Platz has obsessive compulsive disorder. „There are certain sounds, textures or things that will definitely set me off. Hearing more about sensory issues it was like, ok there was something about this I could relate to." He said in an Interview about KultureCity.

- Platz loves food (both eating and preparing it) and has been lucky enough to experience a huge variety of foods from different cultures while traveling with the band, which has led to him falling in love with food even more.

- His brother is a filmmaker, which as a career means that he has traveled all over the world. He even spent some time living in Kazakhstan.

- A picture of his beautiful Bengal cat, Kitty Bang Bang, was used for the album cover of his film score "Carpe Diem".

- He bought a Toyota Corolla when he moved to Las Vegas, as he just wanted a reliable car. Fun fact: There is actually a model of Toyota with the name Platz. It is another name for Toyota Yaris, which was manufactured from 1999 until 2005 in Japan.

- Platz loves to wear "jorts" on stage, a pair of jeans, shortened by himself with scissors or even a knife. He wore them for the band's performance in Kuala Lumpur.

- He can only say two things in German: „Ich mag das" - I like that, and „Es freut mich, Sie kennenzulernen" — nice to meet you. Well,...the only two things that are family friendly.

- When their song „It´s Time" was used in the series „Glee", Platz´s mom was so proud that she took a picture of the tv and sent it to him.

- His biggest cymbal has a name, Beatrice. He even tweeted about it, „Thank you for your hard work, B".

- His grandfather Robert Leroy Platzman was an Associate Professor of Chemistry and Physics at the University of Chicago, as well as other institutions. This could have influenced Platz´s interest in science.

- He sometimes changes his voice to impersonate his own agent during phone interviews.

- Platz is a board member of KultureCity. „My mom is a particular training instructor, and rising up, I noticed the hole in inclusion for these with sensory wants" Platz mentioned in an interview. This explains his passion for the non-profit organization KultureCity, which was founded in 2014.

- Some songs on the album „Mercury" were recorded at his own recording studio „Platzcaster".

Film scoring experiences:

- „Eagles are turning people into Horses" (2009) This was the official selection at the 2010 SlamDance and SXSW Film Festivals.
- „Golden Minutes" - Short film (2009)
- „Cherrylocks and the Three Mexicans" - Short film (2011)
- „Pierre the Pickpocket" (2012)
- „Living with Ebola" - Documentary (2014)
- „Best Friends" (2017)
- „Best Friends Vol. 2" (2018)
- „Carpe Diem" (2020)

As a member of Imagine Dragons, he has also created music for:

„Transformers 4: Age of Extinction", „Suicide Squad", „Believer", „Ralph breaks the Internet", „Kung Fu Panda 3", „Me before you", „Iron Man 3", „Valencia", „The 15:17 to Paris" and other various TV series.

Solo projects:

Platz released Pun and Games, Vol. 1 in May 2012. This Jazz album contains 9 tracks and it was launched by Daniel Platzman Quintet. About 3 years later, in January 2015, he published Pun and Games II: Electric Boogaloo. His second solo project consists of 8 songs and shows once more, that he is still in love with Jazz. Both albums are available for purchase and also on various streaming platforms.

Daniel Platzman´s Charity

KultureCity:

„Make the nevers possible."
The organization provides programs to improve the lives of people with sensory needs or an invisible disability. One of six individuals have these problems. These are individuals with PTSD, autism, dementia or strokes, just to name a few. KultureCity is the nation's leading non-profit on sensory accessibility and acceptance for those with invisible disabilities. For further information, please visit KultureCity:(www.kulturecity.org)

KultureCity

We'd like to introduce to you the charity project of Daniel Platzman and Ben McKee. They are both board members of this organization and Platz was so kind to answer a few questions about KultureCity.

KultureCity isn't very well known to most people. So, would you explain the tasks and targets of your organization in a few words?

We are the worlds leading nonprofit on sensory accessibility and acceptance and inclusion of those with sensory needs/ invisible disabilities. This is essentially 1 in 3 individuals in the world today form those with PTSD, autism, strokes, dementia and many more.

What special accessories do you provide at venues to help people with sensory needs to feel comfortable?

Our sensory inclusive training to all their staff, our sensory bags and sensory rooms. We also integrate the venue with our sensory inclusive app.

What exactly is S.A.V.E.?

It's a mobile sensory room

Let's say someone wants to do a festival and wants to provide a safe space for people with sensory needs, what is the first step?

Reach out to Kulturecity

Is there any way to support your noble cause apart from donations?

Getting venues to be sensory inclusive

Do you provide your service only for Northern America?

No we are in the UK, France, Australia and Canada

Have you ever received feedback from people you have helped?

Yes, we get a ton of feedback.
We are one of the top reviewed non profits in the USA

Thank you for taking the time to answer these questions!
We really appreciate it! If you want to know more about this awesome organization, please visit their homepage:

www.kulturecity.org

Benjamin Arthur McKee

Benjamin Arthur McKee was born on April 7, 1985. He grew up in a home on a little dirt road in a small town called Forestville in Sonoma County, California. He has one sibling, a younger sister named Julia. He has a strong bond with mother nature. Even as a kid, he took care of injured wildlife and helped raise nestlings. He mentioned in an interview, he „has a big place in his heart for animals and for wildlife".

Ben learned to play the acoustic guitar during his childhood and learned to play the violin while in the school orchestra. He started to play the string bass in the 5th grade.

He went to El Molino High School and was a member of the school jazz trio. This experience influenced his decision to apply to the Berklee College of Music in Boston.

A high school classmate of Ben says that: „he was the class clown, he dressed funny and had an awkward laugh and an automatic reflex to make a silly face whenever a camera was pointed at him. He got along with everyone and he had the coolest mom of all of us."

While growing up, loved to listened to Willy Nelson, Prince, and John Hyatt.

While attending Berklee, Ben shared a room with Platz who was also in the same college project as Wayne, for the duration of three years (Guitar Lab).

When Wayne called Ben in 2009, and asked him to join Imagine Dragons, he immediately dropped out of college with only one semester left until graduation, to become a part of the band. He quit college on a whim, and moved to Las Vegas, all without having ever been there before. All from just one phone call with Wayne, that's how much he trusted his friend.

And when the band needed a new drummer, Ben remembered his former roommate, and called Platz to ask if he would also join the band.

Ben - Little Known Facts

- The most annoying thing he does, according to the other members of the band is jumping up and down in an elevator whenever they are in one — in attempts to get it stuck.

- He got impeached as a class president in high school because he used a whole year's worth of Treasury funds to buy milk and cookies for all his classmates.

- He got suspended from school because he didn't want to get a friend in trouble. Ben and a friend had filled balloons with slime at band camp, and threw them up into the vents in the ceiling, so that when they ripped, the slime would fall down and cover the whole floor, causing the teachers to slip and slide around.

- Ben once „borrowed" Wayne´s phone to write an appreciation tweet about himself.

- He was Homecoming King.

- He confessed in an interview that he's not a big fan of the internet.

- He was arrested for public indecency in Las Vegas.

- One night after a gig, Ben tried to scale the walls of a club called Aria in Las Vegas. Unfortunately, he fell down and sprained his ankle. Nontheless, he spent the night dancing in a club, until they shut it down at sunrise.

- Ben disclosed in a tweet that a percussion sound on the track „Only" from the Origins album, was made by slapping his butt.

- When asked by a fan about his favorite slot machine, he answered: „Blackjack really is the game to play".

- Ben has many tattoos, the front of his torso, his arms and his hands, are covered in art. One of his biggest tattoos took a four hour session in Venice, created by the famous artist Dillon Forte. This masterpiece covers his arms from his shoulders, all the way down to his fingertips.

- Ben started a very healthy lifestyle and became a vegan in May 2020, he said on Twitter.

- Ben leaked a song from the Evolve album (Walking The Wire) by sharing it on Twitter before its official release. It was removed after being online for two hours and was officially released a few days later, with the rest of the Evolve album.

- He has an iron stomach. He once won a spicy food eating competition, he drank a whole bottle of pancake syrup and when Dan asked him how many olives he could fit in his mouth, he didn't hesitate to show him that he could fit an entire jarful into his mouth.

- There were once rumors that he had a secret wife in Brazil - which are NOT true!

- While touring with the band Nico Vega, Ben stripped down to his underwear, put on a rubber pig mask, and walked slowly from one side of the stage to the other, in the middle of their performance.

- His favorite game to play is Donkey Kong. (the original arcade game) and according to one of his tweets, he loves donkeys.

- Ben once had a guy lick his face while on stage at the pub "O´Shease" in Las Vegas. Dan had offered this up as the winners prize for a dance contest. Dan thought this was hilarious. Ben... not so much!

- Dan´s sister once kissed Ben on the cheek on stage — she thought it would be fun to try and interrupt his performance.

- He likes to drink hot sauce before going on stage.

- Ben said his worst job was playing jazz at a seafood restaurant, because the manager was constantly shouting at them for playing too loud and interrupting people´s conversations.

- He once drank too much Aquavit in Norway and left the club with two tall women. He was gone for six hours and he still can't remember what happened!

- His ancestors were from Ireland, Scotland and Germany.

- Ben had a cockatiel named Hootie as a child.

- He is a big fan of the San Francisco 49ers American football (NFL) team.

- Ben paid his tuition fee with financial assistance from a California State scholarship for talented chemistry students.

- Ben´s grandmother was involved in Planned Parenthood and Ben delivered groceries to people suffering with HIV and Aids with his family. This taught him, from a very young age, the importance of social commitment.

- He loves cooking and recommends it to everyone.

- Ben never, ever gets nervous before going on stage.

- He got his first tattoo in March 2018 and has had a lot more since. He still doesn't think he's finished adding body art, yet.

- He claims that shortbread is his favorite kind of Christmas cookie.

- The McKee family motto, according to Wayne, is „Better a church burnt down, than a drop of liquor spilled".

- On Twitter, he said that his favorite Christmas movie is „It's A Wonderful Life".... Apparently it makes him cry every year.

- Ben has a big heart and volunteers at his local animal shelter whenever he's home.

- He knows how to knit socks.

- One of Ben´s greatest loves is his dog, a beagle named, Sammich. He even embroidered her face on one of his bass straps for and Sammich has her own Instagram account!

- Ben´s life motto is „Be kind. Always."

- According to Dan, Ben has a green thumb.... He used to have an organic garden in the backyard of his apartment in Los Angeles.

- He tweeted in May 2021: „Some of my favorite summer memories are of rafting down the rogue river with my family" so he's obviously a nature lover.

- Ben loves „waffles and mochi"

- In an interview in November 2021, he mentioned that a new tattoo on his back is in progress.

Ben McKee´s Charities

KultureCity:

„Make the nevers possible."
The organization provides programs to improve the lives of people with sensory needs or an invisible disability. One of six individuals have these problems. These are individuals with PTSD, autism, dementia or strokes just to name a few.
KultureCity is the nations leading non-profit on sensory accessibility and acceptance for those with invisible disabilities.
For further information, please visit: www.kulturecity.org

Today I Give:
Daily Donations of $1,000 throughout a whole year:

On Feb. 16th, 2021, Ben posted on Twitter:
„Life has been incredibly generous to me. Never did I think that my journey would take me from a dead-end, dirt road in a tiny town in Northern California to some of the biggest stages, in front of the best fans, as a member of one of the most successful bands in the world. The past year has been a particularly challenging time for a lot of people. The organizations that fight to support and protect the most vulnerable of us have been pushed beyond their limits. I have set aside $365,000 and over the next year I will be giving away $1,000 a day to a cause or organization that has been working to protect and support the rights and livelihoods of those that have been most threatened. I will document my donations here, beginning tomorrow."

Please check on Ben´s Twitter or Instagram account for details about all the organizations he has supported.

Women's Audio Mission - Changing The Face Of Sound (WAM)

Ben tweeted on March 1, 2022, that he has become a proud board member of this organization. He was inspired to join WAM after witnessing the lack of diversity that is pervasive throughout the recording industry and the power that a motivated group of people coming together can have to create positive change. Ben lives in the Bay Area and is thrilled to be a part of an organization fighting to change a global industry he works in, from a home base in the community where he lives. For further information please visit WAM´s website: womensaudiomission.org

Wonderful, Peculiar Bassist

So you want me to tell you about Benjamin McKee
And that's a little bit of a challenge for me, because
He's lots of peculiar, wonderful things, and
I'm not sure where to start, or what to say, but
I'll try my best for you, anyway

I could start by saying. . .

Ben was a Julia-Child-instead-of-Nickolodeon-kid
Always getting in interesting trouble, and
He still does that now, to dismay or delight
Though jumping in elevators. . . maybe isn't so bright

Oh, and once, he. . .

Was impeached as class president, see
He spent the whole budget on milk and cookies
And that sounds like a fine president to me, but
I guess the school board disagreed

And that brings me to say. . .

His culinary skills are excellent, really
He challenged his local bakery making chocolate chip cookies
And he also drinks hot sauce before going on stage, but
He's a fascinating guy, in fascinating ways

Another thing to mention, is. . .

He's a legend with the bass, a master of his craft
He knows rhyme and rhythm, and the power they will have
Music is his passion, a passion he honors with grace, and
He's a glowing inspiration to anyone else with passions that they
chase

I stumble with my words; I do hope this is clear
If you want to know Ben, this is what you should hear:

He listens to the dreamers, and believes in what they do
Because once, years ago, he was a dreamer too, and
I don't know if he felt it, or if he somehow knew, that
All that he'd become, and all that he would do

And while that's something I like to ponder,
it doesn't matter, see
But what does, is. . .

Ben is the kindest guy you'll meet, and he always takes a stand
He fights for what's important, and he's an uplifting,
amazing man
He's strange but in the best way, he's charming and unique, and
And full of the wonderful, peculiar things, that
That make him Ben McKee

Daniel Coulter Reynolds

Daniel Coulter Reynolds was born on July 14, 1987, in Las Vegas, Nevada. He's the seventh of nine children born to Christene and Ronald Reynolds. He has seven brothers and one sister. Growing up, Dan´s Mom insisted he should take piano lessons until the age of 16. She believed that it helped develop the brain and would therefore be good for him when he was learning and studying.

While growing up he listened to Hip Hop and Rap Artists such as OutKast, 2Pac, and the Notorious B.I.G. He also listened to Alternative, Grunge and Rock Artists such as REM, Nirvana, Pearl Jam, Alanis Morissette, Paul Simon, Harry Nilsson, Rolling Stones and G.Love & Special Sauce (this was the first concert he ever went to).

Dan refers to himself as the black sheep of the family, always getting into trouble. All his brothers became doctors and lawyers, while he was getting the worst grades. In middle school he had braces on his teeth, suffered from acne, and he also felt quite alone and lost. Because of this, combined with having a difficult time at school in general, he started writing his feelings down and turned them into songs, at the young age of thirteen.

After finishing high school, he applied (like his six other brothers before him) to BYU. He had to work hard to get into the university, which involved extra after school work. One week before he was due to start his studies at BYU, he met with an LDS bishop. He told the bishop that he had sex with his girlfriend of four years, which led to Dan being kicked out of BYU before the term had even started. This proved to be a trigger point in his life. He felt like the whole community was judging him. And this was the first time he really experienced depression.

So in the end, he stayed at home and went to UNLV (University of Nevada, Las Vegas). When alone, without his friends who had all gone to BYU, he dejectedly wandered from class to class with a hoodie on, feeling very depressed for the whole semester.

At the age of nineteen, Dan went on a two year LDS mission to several states - Omaha, Nebraska, being one of them. In an interview, he said: „It was such a growing experience for me, and it humbled me and made me realize that the World is a lot bigger than where you're raised. There are people with so many more problems than you and it makes your problems seem really small."

After finishing the mission, he finally made it to Brigham Young University (BYU). There, he met Andrew Tolman and the two of them decided to create music together. Dan was convinced that he had to do music when he and a few guys from campus (Andrew Tolman included) won the „Battle of the Bands" contest at his college in 2008. This made him realize that he seriously wanted to form a band. It was also the first time the name Imagine Dragons was used. Later that year, they also won the „Utah Valley University's Got Talent" competition.

Dan decided to drop out of college to pursue music as a career. In an interview, Dan explained: „I wasn't happy or interested in my major. Music was the only thing I'd done since I was twelve, that I really loved and I couldn't see myself doing anything else. It was a difficult decision. The last thing you want to tell your parents is.... 'I'm dropping out of college to be in a rock band.'"

At the age of twenty-one, Dan began to experience debilitating pain that forced him to cancel a few shows. He said: „I couldn't get on stage. I couldn't move, I couldn't sleep at night, I couldn't perform without standing perfectly still. I couldn't sit down for more than half an hour".

After consulting many doctors, he took some the advice from his sibling to go and see a rheumatologist. After years of pain, he finally got the right diagnosis... Ankylosing spondylitis, a chronic inflammatory condition of the joints. He was given a treatment plan of healthy eating, yoga and staying active.This helped him a lot.

He kept his disease as a secret for years, but finally at a sold out show at Leeds Arena in West Yorkshire, England, he shared his diagnosis with fans.

In Dec 2009 during a show at the now closed Waste Space Place at Hard Rock Cafe in Los Angeles, Dan Reynolds met his future wife Aja Volkman, lead singer of the band Nico Vega.

Dan said in an interview: "It seemed that music was the only link we had. But as we got to know each other on a more personal level, we found that we had so many similarities in our hearts that it was scary. I never had met someone who I connected with so instantly. Everything about her captivated me. I needed to know her." Their first conversation started off very philosophically with Dan asking about her beliefs. She spoke about giving up Scientology and Dan discussed doubting his Mormon roots.

A few months later, Dan bought a bunch Christmas lights with the very last of the money he had in his wallet and with the lights, he spelled out „Will you marry me?" on the grass. A friend of his lit them up, as Dan and Aja looked down on the lights from above. He got down on one knee and asked her to marry him. They got married on March 5, 2011.

The couple announced in April 2018, that they were getting divorced after seven years of marriage.

After not speaking to each other for months, and having never signed the divorce papers, they started dating again. Aja confirmed in January 2019 that they were officially back together. The couple were so intent on building up and strengthening their relationship that they started going to marriage counseling.

Even though progress had been made, Aja refused to put her first wedding ring back on. So in true Dan romantic style, he got a new ring, and on Christmas of 2019, in front of the family's tree, he got down on one knee and asked her to marry him again. Aja´s reply was „The answer has always been yes."

The couple have 4 children together: Arrow Eve (August 18, 2012), Gia James and Coco Rae (Twins) (March 28, 2017) and Valentine Reynolds(October 1, 2019).

Dan - Little Known Facts

- Dan is extremely claustrophobic, this is because when he was little, one of his brothers locked him in a tiny box while doing a magic trick.

- Dan received the BSA´s top rank, Eagle Scout, in 2004 as a member of a scout unit, chartered to the LDS church in Nevada.

- He bought Goldie Hawn and Kurt Russells vacation getaway oceanfront house on Malibu´s Broad Beach.

- He knows how to code in Unity and C#. After taking a few courses, he started making small computer games to practice. He also wants to create a game with his brother Mac.

- Dan has been diagnosed with stress-related high blood pressure and has even woken up in the morning with a locked jaw because of it. He also suffers from Ulcerative Colitis.

- In the early years of the band, Dan had surgery to remove a huge polyp on his vocal cords. He had been singing from the wrong place, so he took singing lessons to help spare his voice.

- After performing Radioactive in 2013 in Berlin, Dan shattered two bones in his right hand by punching the bass drum extremely hard, and ended up going to the ER to have a cast put on. Two years later, he got a hairline fracture on the same arm during his performance in Oberhausen, Germany. Seems, Germany isn't a good place for him to perform....

- In 2021, he started doing Brazilian Jiu-Jitsu in addition to his regular training. His trainer, Neale Hoerle, is a 1st degree Jiu Jitsu Black Belt holder and also a certified personal trainer (NASM-CPT). Neale, along with Edward Yang and Dan´s personal trainer Brad Feinberg, helps Dan stay in shape and keep his AS under control.

- Dan´s favorite albums are „Graceland" from Paul Simon and Harry Nilsson´s "Nilsson Schmilsson".

- In 2014, Dan and the band were on their way back to Las Vegas, when suddenly their plane jolted and began losing altitude. „All the people around me were freaking out, but I was just sitting there, and I had no reaction. And that actually scared me, because I felt like I didn't care — if the plane went down right then, I just didn't care. That was the moment for me, where I talked to my wife and said „All right. It´s time to go see a therapist."

- He hates toe-socks — „No one wants to see your toes".

- To wean his daughter Arrow off of her pacifier at the age of two, he told her that they had to give it to another sad girl that needed it. And because she has such a big heart, Arrow said: „Okay, that makes sense."

- Dan has imitated their manager Mac on the phone several times to get a table in a fully booked restaurant. That didn't go down well with Mac.

- Dan and Aja wrote the song „Bad Liar" from the album "Origins" about one month before they separated.

- Together with Steve Angello, Dan released „Someone Else" on January 22, 2016.

- Apparently, Aja, Dan´s wife is one of very few people who know what Imagine Dragons is actually an anagram of.

- During a concert once, a girl in the audience showed Dan that she got the lyrics from the song „Drive" tattooed on her arm. It was this that made him realize just how important it is to think about the lyrics that he writes.

- He owns a custom made 1967 Ford Mustang.

- After the Night Visions tour, and coming back from Hong Kong, where the band had been to the world premiere of „Transformers - Age of Extinction", Dan´s voice had suffered so much that he had to go on steroids.

- Dan and Aja created a musical project called "Egyptian" together.

- One thing that Dan says he's proud of, is being kissed on the cheek by Ringo Star at the Grammys.

- Dan had to give himself bi-weekly injections of an immunosuppressant, this made him more susceptible to sickness on the road, but it was worth it to be able to perform despite his AS disease.

- When performing live, Dan emotionally goes back to the feeling he had when he wrote the song, so the emotions he shows on stage are real. He has said that he can't fake it.

- Dan´s ancestors are from Switzerland, Aja´s are from Italy.

- After performing with Imagine Dragons at The Joint in the Hard Rock Hotel on Dec 30, 2013, Dan ended up DJ´ing at Body English, a nearby after-hours club.

- He says his first french kiss was really bad. It was with a girl when he was in 7th grade.

- A past job that Dan hated doing, was when he worked for a law firm and had to call people who were in debt and try to convince them to pay, saying he would have to have their car repossessed if they didn't.

- He formed "Night Street Records", a subsidiary of Interscope Records. The first artist Dan signed to Night Street was K. Flay. Benson Boone, an American TikTok star and participant of American Idol, signed in October 2021

- He received the Songwriters Hall of Fame „Hal David Starlight Award" in 2014.

- Dan wrote „It´s Time" at the age of 21 when he was thinking about dropping out of college.

- He made the film „Believer" about the LGTBQ+ community and the Mormon church. Dan even created the song „Skipping Stones" for the documentary and released it on June 21, 2018. A second track "So Many Voices" is unreleased, although a snippet was used in „Believer".

- In younger years, Dan wanted to be an FBI agent, so he used to follow police sirens to the scene of a crime.

- He collaborated with the British artist Yungblud for the song „Original me". The single was released on Oct 8, 2019.

- For the Black Lives Matter (BLM) movement, Dan collaborated with Tom Morello and Shea Diamond and released the single „Stand up". All proceeds are donated to these organizations: NAACP, Know Your Rights Camp, Southern Poverty Law Center and Marsh P. Johnson Institute. The single was released July 2, 2020.

- On Feb. 21st 2021, Dan bought his childhood home from his parents and donated it to the charity organization, Encircle. He also collaborated with Apple's CEO Tim Cook, and Utah Jazz owner Ryan Smith. Together, they donated 4 millions US dollars to Encircle, who provide safe homes for LGTBQ+ youth.

- Dan Reynolds was the first one to use a on a new vending machine that was set up in Las Vegas in November 2021. It allows people to donate for local and international non-profits. The „Giving Machine" is located in Summerlin, Las Vegas.

Dan Reynolds´ Charities

LoveLoud Music Festival:

LOVELOUD was founded in 2017 by Dan Reynolds to help ignite the relevant and vital conversation of what it means to unconditionally love, understand, accept, and support LGBTQ+ youth in an effort to keep families together. LOVELOUD is the catalyst for bringing communities together to start the conversation and celebrate individuality. Talking, sharing and showing the realities of what teens in our society face daily is where it all begins. Proceeds from the festival are donated to LGBTQ support groups like The Trevor Project, Encircle, Tegan and Sara Foundation, GLAAD, and a lot more.

Don Argott directed the film „Believer" which follows Mormon Dan Reynolds for one whole year, documenting his attempt to change the way the Mormon Church treats its LGTBQ members. But „Believer" also focuses on the suicide rate in the community, which has skyrocketed in the last decade. The HBO film had it´s world premier at the 2018 Sundance Film Festival.

Ankylosing Spondylitis:

Dan Reynolds (as well as four of his brothers) has suffered from this disease since his early twenties. He was undiagnosed for years and he wants to shine a light on this often misdiagnosed disease. Dan has joined the This AS Life campaign, which is a partnership between global health care company Novartis and the Spondylitis Association of America, and is now connecting with others with AS via a series of webisodes of This AS Life Live at ThisASLife.com. During the episodes he interviews people living with AS about their specific diets, exercise and pain-management regimens.

He also launched a website to make it easier for people to get the right diagnosis by taking a short self test to find out if they are affected by the disease AS. The Website is: www.monsterpainintheas.com

LOVELOUD

The LoveLoud charity organization, which was founded 2017 by Dan Reynolds focuses on supporting LGTBQ+ youth. The LoveLoud festival held in Salt Lake City, Utah is an important part of the foundation. At this awesome festival, people are able to speak their truth and spread the message of love and acceptance. Apart from that, many artists and bands perform on stage. All proceeds of this festival go to different organizations like Encircle, GLAAD, The Tegan and Sara Foundation, The Trevor Project and many other remarkable charities. We had the opportunity to speak to Clarissa Savage, executive director of LoveLoud.

Is Mr. Reynolds still actively involved in the planning and execution of the festival or does his work consist mainly of representative activities these days?

Dan is still the chair of the LOVELOUD Board, attends every meeting, and helps execute all aspects of the foundation and festival.

Every large-scale cultural event, including LoveLoud, had to be cancelled last year due to the pandemic. So, after a hiatus of one year (at least) will there be any big changes or new developments for the festival when it resumes?

Because of the financial burden and time it takes to plan a festival, we have decided to push until 2022, but can't wait for the festival to be come back bigger than ever!

In your opinion, what might be interesting to know about LoveLoud that isn't commonly known?

We are first and foremost a foundation and secondly a music festival. We are constantly trying to remain present in the community even when we are unable to have a music festival!

About the festival in general: How many people are involved in the organization of LoveLoud?

I am currently the only employee of LOVELOUD. We have a board of 9 people and advisory board of another 10 people, but besides that it's completely volunteer based!

Sadly, there are huge problems for LGTBQ+ youth in every part of the world. Are there any plans to expand the festival to places outside of Utah, maybe even outside of North America?

We would love that eventually. That's the goal, LOVELOUD is so necessary in so many places around the world and we'd love to make that happen!

We'd love to hear one or two incidents that happened during LoveLoud... Something touching, heartwarming or just something funny? Please give us a small peek behind the scenes.

I think the most important moments at LOVELOUD happen when a child is able to come out to their family at LOVELOUD. I have also witnessed many special moments between Tyler Glenn and LGBTQ+ youth in Utah and hearing how by learning of Tyler's story through Believer it has saved their own lives!

Is there any possibility to support LoveLoud apart from donations?

We have merch on our site which is a great way to support the foundation as well as spread our messaging! Follow us on socials and share our messaging, that is always helpful!

Thank you for this amazing interview and your time!

You'll find more information on LoveLoudfest.com and don´t forget to follow them on social media.

The Beginning Of Imagine Dragons

After Dan had completed his mission in Nebraska, he formed a band together with Andrew Tolman (one of Wayne´s best friends) at BYU. Imagine Dragons was born. The band consisted of Aurora Florence (Violin, Vocals), Dave Lemke (Guitar), Andrew Beck (Keyboard, Vocals), Andrew Tolman (Drums) and of course Dan Reynolds (Vocals). Aurora Florence and Andrew Beck left after less than a year with the band, which led to Andrew Tolman recruiting his wife, Brittany Tolman. Dave Lemke then left the band in 2009.

Dan met Wayne after hearing him perform at Club Velour in Provo, Utah and approached him to talk about his musical interests. Dan invited him to join his band (Imagine Dragons needed a guitarist after Dave Lemke had left) and asked him if he could move to Las Vegas. Dan dropped out of college (for the second time) to start a career in music. They had only known each other for about a month when Wayne decided to move to Las Vegas to support Dan and become a member of Imagine Dragons. When they needed a bass player, Wayne called Ben and invited him to join the band.

They rented an old house and started to practice together, with the line up consisted of Dan, Andrew, Brittany, Wayne and Ben for their first gigs. One of Dan´s older brothers, Robert had some experience in the music industry from managing The Killers and also helping Neon Trees find success, so he was on hand to give them any advice that they needed.

For the first few years they played a lot of empty venues, one of them being in Salt Lake City where they played in front of just five people (and one of them was the bartender) and this was one of the better gigs.... At their first performance in L.A. the only person there to watch them was their manager, Mac Reynolds.

Money was tight for the whole band, they literally lived on Ramen, Toast with Nutella, and Rice and Beans. Andrew and Brittany worked part time for Robert Reynolds, a lawyer and one of Dan´s brothers, to earn some money, and Wayne´s parents helped support him financially. They earned a small amount of money from gigs and playing live at casinos, their set was made up of half cover songs, and the other half original songs.

The band said yes to every single opportunity that came their way, anything that would bring in some money. This included performing at Bar-mitzvahs, birthday parties and even playing for the opening of a mall.

By 2011, Imagine Dragons could sell out clubs like the „Velour" in Provo,Utah with a capacity of 300 people. Sadly, the progress was a little too slow for Brittany and Andrew Tolman.... They decided to leave the band and go back to college (which they had quit to establish the band with Dan). At this stage, Wayne was also seriously thinking about leaving the band, but luckily his wife and his parents managed to convince him to stay.

When Andrew Tolman left, Imagine Dragons needed a new drummer, and so they reached out to Daniel Platzman, who was playing jazz in New York at the time. After Ben called him, he left New York and joined the band. So Platz completed the ensemble and they moved from Las Vegas to Los Angeles. At this point, the band had already released a few self produced EP´s. One day, an assistant gave AlexDaKid one of the EP´s to listen to. AlexDaKid liked it, and contacted Mac Reynolds, the bands´ manager, and told him that he wanted to work together.

Alex „da Kid" Grant invited Imagine Dragons to come to Los Angeles to write songs with him, which they did solidly until Interscope Chairman, Jimmy Iovine, asked them to sign their contracts. On November 17, 2011, Imagine Dragons, a band of three years by then, officially announced that they'd signed a co-deal with Interscope Records and KIDinaKORNER.

When it came to recording their first full length album, Night Visions, they rented an apartment in L.A., where the band was still touring and performing in clubs on the West coast. During this period, Dan was constantly writing and spent a lot of time in the studio. When Imagine Dragons released their debut album, they were hoping it would have 20,000 - 30,000 sales in the first week. Instead, to their amazement over 80,000 copies were sold. And the rest, as they say, is history.

Extended Play (EP)

Speak To Me - EP (Self release at September 11, 2008)
The name Speak To Me was given by the community, the album is just an untitled collection of unreleased demos. As the band consisted of completely different members, some people don't consider this album as a part of Imagine Dragons discography.

Imagine Dragons - EP (Self-released at September 1, 2009) This Extended Play was recorded at the Killers´ Battle Born Studios. The cover of this album is an autostereogram, this means that if you stare at the cover of the EP, your eyes blur and then they slowly focus again, a 3D dragon appears.

Hell And Silence - EP (Self-released at June 1, 2010) Although the song „Selene" was also used in their first full length album, Night Visions, the EP version is slightly different. Hell And Silence was also recorded at the Battle Born Studios.

It's Time - EP (Self-released at March 12, 2011)
Many of the songs of this EP were later used on the album Night Visions. The band recorded this EP in Studio X at the Palms Hotel and Casino in fall 2010.

Continued Silence - EP (released by KIDinaKORNER, Interscope, Feb. 14th, 2012)
This was their first EP which was released after signing the record deal with Interscope Records.

Staring as the stars parade
Are they telling me it´s gonna be okay?
You´ve gotta live your life
While your blood is boiling
Those doors won't open
While you stand and watch them

Cha-Ching (Till We Grow Older)
Night Visions

Brittany & Andrew
Tolman

Dan Reynolds founded the band in his college days with completely different members. Two of them were Brittany and Andrew Tolman. Brittany played the keyboard and was a backing vocalist and Andrew was the drummer of the band. Together they released four EP´s (Speak To Me, Imagine Dragons EP, Hell And Silence and It´s Time) and performed at many different locations. The couple left the band due to personal reasons and that was the moment when Daniel Platzman joined.

Let's shed a light on former Imagine Dragons members Brittany and Andrew here:

Andrew Tolman was born on January 9, 1986, in American Fork, Utah. He attended BYU and married Brittany Tolman during this period of time. After being the drummer for Imagine Dragons for a few years (2008 - 2011), he and Brittany decided to leave the band. Andrew joined alt rock band, The Moth & The Flame as a drummer in 2012 and he is still making music with them.

Brittany Tolman also attended Brigham Young University (BYU) and became best friends with Alexandra Hall. Brittany married Andrew Tolman in her junior year at BYU, and became a member of Imagine Dragons in 2009. She replaced Aurora Florence on the keyboard and as backing vocalist for the band. After two years, she left the band and decided to concentrate on her personal life.

And here are some interesting facts about Brittany & Andrew Tolman:

- Andrew Tolman was one of Wayne´s best childhood friends in American Fork. So it was only a matter of time until Alexandra met Wayne in this friend circle. They fell in love and when they decided to spend the rest of their lives together, Brittany was Alex´s maid of honor — and Andrew had the honor of being Wayne´s best man. So, Brittany and Andrew were not only important members of the new found group Imagine Dragons, but they also played an important role in the private life of guitarist, Wayne Sermon.

- Brittany played keys and was backing vocalist for the Killers album, "Big Talk" released in 2011.

- In 2014-2016, Brittany was the singer of the band, Mount Saint, an indie pop group. Andrew supported the band as studio drummer. Clint Holgate, lead vocalist of Mount Saint, co-wrote the Imagine Dragons song Cha-Ching. Mount Saint performed a few times at Velour in Utah, a music venue which ID also performed at several times. In 2016, Mount Saint broke up and split into 2 different bands: Tolman and Strange Joy.

- In 2016, the pop duo Tolman, which consisted of Andrew and Brittany, released two singles „Chaperone" and „Freeway". The track „Chaperone" was co-produced by Daniel Wayne Sermon.

- At the launch of Imagine Dragons album „Origins" (November 2018), Andrew and Brittany made a guest appearance and performed their classic song, "Destination" along with the band.

- Andrew Tolman co-wrote a few songs from Imagine Dragons´ fifth studio album "Mercury Act 1 & 2". In 2021, together with the band, he co-wrote the songs "Monday", "Giants", "It´s OK", „Higher Ground", „I´m Happy", „Younger" and „They Don´t Know You Like I Do".

Night Visions

Was released September 4, 2012, under the label Interscope - KIDinaKORNER. The album featured the following singles: It's Time, Radioactive, Hear Me, Demons and On Top of the World. Night Visions saw several different versions released across multiple countries.

The standard version featured 11 tracks, but there were also bonus tracks for iTunes, Spotify, Best Buy and Target. They also released a North American deluxe edition. The artwork for the cover is by the Russian artist Eugen Soloviev.

For their debut album, Night Visions, Imagine Dragons had more than 100 demos to choose from. Some of the song were recorded on Dan´s laptop and not in the studio, because he liked how they sounded.

While recording Night Visions, the band ended up working 18-20 hours per day because they needed to get maximum efficiency out of each day in the studio, where renting studio time is extremely expensive and they were low on funds.

As well as Dan, Platz, Ben and Wayne, Andrew and Brittany Tolman also contributed in a few songs on the album: It's Time, Amsterdam, Hear Me, Cover Up, America, The River, Selene and I Don't Mind.

Promotion

- In the first week of it´s release, the album could be purchased for $5 from Amazon. Other similar deals could be found in the iTunes Store, and with an in store coupon.

- The band also released a documentary about the <u>Making of Night Visions</u>, it debuted at the end of 2012 on VH1 Palladia.

- The song Amsterdam was released exclusively as a free download via iTunes as "Single of the week".

Music videos

"It's Time"

This was the first music video from Imagine Dragons.
The video depicts an end of world type scene. The band walk through a barren wasteland, one of them opens a box he had been carrying. They take a glowing orb out of the box, dig a hole in the ground with their bare hands and drop it into the soil. After Dan yells at the band to run, there´s a huge explosion, and the band is thrown into the air. Finally, the grey and ominous looking sky begins to part, and the sunlight shines through.

A video by director Matt Eastin and Isaac Halasima is also available for this song. Corey Fox, owner of the famous club Velour in Utah, was responsible for furnishing „It´s Time". (Acoustic From The Occidental Saloon)

"On Top Of The World"

This video is about the conspiracy theory regarding the Moon landing. It is said that the landing never actually happened and that film director Stanley Kubrick faked it. So the music video is full of allusions to Kubrick´s films (like The Shining or 2001). The moon scene was shot in the BYU TV studios and seven tons of crushed limestone had to be carried to the film set. Have fun discovering all the hidden !! 200!! Easter eggs in this video.

The video took 2 days to shoot, in a small town in Utah. A few fun facts: The boy on the bobby car is Matt Eastin´s nephew, and the director himself taped „That's one false step for a man, one giant deceit for mankind" at 4 am on his karaoke machine in his basement. This phrase was used in the music video when the astronauts set foot on the moon.

"Radioactive"

A girl tries to save her friends (the band) from the perils of a sinister, underground puppet fighting ring, with the help of her pink teddy bear and it´s magical powers.

Dan said in an MTV interview "We read through a ton of scripts from really talented directors, and we came across one that stood out to us in particular, because it put into visuals the general theme of the song, which is kind of an empowering song about an awakening, but it did it in a way that was very different. A lot of people probably see a post-apocalyptic world when they hear Radioactive, understandably, but we wanted to deliver something that was maybe a little different from that.... A lot different from that."

"Demons"

This video is a mix of a live concert, and a companion narrative. Their live performance in Las Vegas at The Joint is interrupted with footage about different characters and their struggles in life. Like a woman who has just lost her mother, a man with Marfan syndrome, a boy who's abused by his father and a military veteran suffering with PTSD. This narrative shows that it is impossible to see into one's (damaged) soul. The video ends with a dedication to Tyler Robinson, a big fan of Imagine Dragons who died March 4, 2013. The band founded the Tyler Robinson Foundation to commemorate him.

The video surpassed 1 billion views on YouTube in July 2022.

Tour

The band did a 40 date tour to promote Night Visions. It was called The Fall Tour 2012, and they performed as an opening act for „Awolnation".

In 2013, the Night Visions World Tour began, this consisted of 130 headline dates and 50 festivals. The tour started on February 8, 2013, in Tempe, AZ. They performed their last concert of the tour on December 13, 2013, in Bournemouth, England. It was then announced that there were to be some additional concert dates (Into the Night Tour). This tour started February 8, 2014, in Boise, ID and ended March 15, 2014, in Denver, CO. The band was accompanied on this tour by Ryan Walker on the keyboards, guitar, and percussion. Opening Act for Imagine Dragons´ „Into the Night" concerts were The Naked and Famous, X Ambassadors and Nico Vega.

Surprising facts

There are often surprises when it comes to the popularity of songs from an album, which aren't chosen to be released as a single. The following songs from Night Visions had a tremendous numbers of people streaming them on Spotify

Bleeding Out   Tiptoe   Nothing Left To Say/Rocks

Bleeding Out is the most popular album track by Imagine Dragons. It even peaked at number 30 on the Billboard Rock Song Chart on August 6, 2013.

Nearly 8 years after it made its first appearance, **Nothing Left To Say** received a huge amount of attention when the band released an Art Film to accompany the song.

When you listen to Imagine Dragons song **Cha Ching** backwards, you can hear Dan sing „There is no anagram" at 1:07 min.

The very first demo of **It´s Time** included the lyrics of Amsterdam mixed with the chorus of It´s Time. Eventually, the band decided to rewrite the lyrics. So originally the song Amsterdam, came from It´s Time.

Additional releases

Before releasing another full length album, the band brought out a few EP´s and Singles. The first single was released shortly after the launch of Night Visions on September 25 , 2012.
The song Lost Cause is one of ID´s darkest songs and part of the Frankenweenie Unleashed! Album.

The EP „**The Archive**" was only released digitally in the US iTunes Store and featured Round And Round, The River, America, Selene and My Fault. It was released on February 12, 2013. After the band launched the Deluxe version of Night Visions, this EP was taken down permanently after being in the iTunes store for 48 days.

Imagine Dragons first live album was released in April 2013. „**Live at Independent Records**" which was recorded live at a record store in Denver, Colorado. This session was recorded about one month after Dan´s surgery on his vocal cords and although the doctor advised him not to sing, he did the gig anyway because he didn't want to disappoint their fans. Apart from the Introduction, the album consisted only of three tracks: It's Time, Radioactive and Hear Me.

On April 30, 2013, Imagine Dragons released the song „Ready, Aim, Fire" which was part of the „Iron Man 3" Soundtrack.

The band released another live album in May 2013: „**iTunes Session EP**". It featured acoustic versions of It's Time, Radioactive, Amsterdam, 30 Lives and Destination.

The band recorded their third live album „**Night Visions Live**" during their Night Visions Tour stop at the Red Rock Amphitheater on May 16, 2013. The DVD album, which contains a mix of live Concert, Behind the scenes, and "Making of" footage, was released on February 25, 2014.

Additional Releases

On August 15, 2014, a DVD of their concert at the Lowlands Festival in The Netherlands released. The DVD „**Live at Lowlands**" contains Fallen, TipToe, Hear Me, It's Time, Amsterdam, Rocks, Who We Are, On Top Of The World, Demons and Radioactive.

The band created a track for the Original Soundtrack of „Transformers: Age of Extinction". Battle Cry, which was included in the film, it was released as a promotional single on June 2, 2014. The song was also a part of the Super Deluxe version of Smoke + Mirrors.

Another song from the same Transformers film soundtrack is All For You, which was digitally released in December 2020.

Tessa, the name of a piece of music which was used as an intro for the song Trouble, during the Smoke + Mirrors tour, was also used in the Original Soundtrack for „Transformers: Age of Extinction". Dan´s beautiful vocals combined with Daniel Platzman´s soaring viola create this stunningly atmospheric song.

„Warriors" was made in support of „League of Legends World Championship" and was released on September 18, 2014.

Yeah, life is just perspective
Laughing when you´ve wrecked it
Smiling when you kept it together
You weathered the storm
At the end of the play, you sang all the way
Doesn't matter how off-key
If you did it your way

Symphony
Mercury Act 1 & 2

Ryan Walker

He was known as a very passionate touring member for Imagine Dragons during their Night Visions Tour, but playing instruments was only a small part of his many jobs on tour. There is so much more to learn about him.

Ryan Walker is originally from Vista, near San Diego, California, USA. He started making music at the age of twelve with his band Monkey Meets The Banana. His older brother was the manager of the band Korn, and they were the ones who taught him how to play guitar. This was the first instrument he learned and soon after he learned to play other instruments as well.

Ryan was a member of a high school punk band and he was very fervent about that... he even dyed his hair blue and red and bleached it! At the age of fourteen he played his first live show. When asked about his inspiration, he named the band Korn and The Strokes, and also expressed his love for Michael Jackson, whose album was the first that he ever owned. His passion for music was even apparent at a young age when Ryan created fake backstage passes along with his bandmates just to see every show at a festival in San Diego.

He moved from San Diego to L.A. and met Dan and the band at the South by Southwest Festival (SXSW) in March 2010 in Austin, Texas. Impressed by their performance Ryan told Dan that he would love to be part of the band if the opportunity would arose one day. Just a few months later, Dan reached out to him on Facebook and hired him as tour manager. Soon the band figured out that he could also play instruments very well, and so he ended up as not only their tour manager, but also chauffeur of the Dragon Wagon at night, selling merch, and performing on stage with them too. He definitely payed his dues...

"Dreamers", Ryan's project, was literally his second love while touring with Imagine Dragons. Dreamers is a collective of musicians from different bands. Ryan's brother is also involved in the project. He works as a director and did "The Dreamers" video in a single take, Ryan said on Reddit.

And here are some interesting facts about Ryan Walker:

- Ryan's last job before Dan reached out to him was quite uncommon: He put on a Fashion trade show!

- Performing on stage, he is in his own world, giving 110%. He barely looks up to see the fans, he only slowly learned to soak in the energy and enjoy the love and attention of the fans.

- And this is the story behind Ryans nickname Wolf: He was driving the tour bus at night and when he pulled over to check emails and messages, the light of the cell phone screen mirrored in his eyes. Dan, who was sleeping in the back of the tourbus, woke up, saw his shiny eyes in the rearview mirror and said, „Man, you kinda look like a wolf with your eyes."

- Platz is one of his best friends and the only one who he won't prank. Platz and Ryan share a close bond. They would both rather talk sports than go to bars!

- One day, the band pranked him by hanging up a poster of him in front of a venue. The poster said „Ryan Walker is banned from this venue. Warning: He is extremely volatile. If seen, detain and escort him with extreme prejudice"... and the security guard took it very seriously.

- He loves peanut butter and chocolate, drinks his coffee with a bit of sugar and cream, names Tiptoe as his favorite song to play live and considers ID as his family.

- Ryan has been thrown into a fountain in Switzerland by his bandmates (what a nice and loving family!)

- When asked about his funniest memory of the Night Visions tour, Ryan described this prank: Ben went out in his underwear on stage during the opening acts final song (Atlas Genius, X Ambassadors,..)

- His favorite opening band for Imagine Dragons was X Ambassadors.

Smoke + Mirrors

After choosing the perfect songs from about 120 demos, the band released their second studio album "Smoke + Mirrors", which was launched at the House of Vans, London, in 2015.

Dan said: „We wrote a lot of it while we were on the road, while everything was changing in our lives. Our lives have been completely flipped upside down in the last couple of years. In very great ways. But when things change, there's the high-highs and the low-lows. So this record kind of captures a lot of the emotions I was feeling during all of this. And I still am feeling. There's moments of gratitude, there's moments of summer, there are some darker moments in there... but at the end of the day, it´s really a record of kind of a celebration of life."

Smoke + Mirrors was released on February 17, 2015, in the US. This masterpiece was self produced and recorded at Imagine Dragons´ own studio in Las Vegas. The title track Smoke and Mirrors was written by Dan, late at night in his hotel room, while he was going through a low phase of his life. The songs I Bet My Life, Gold and Shots were all chosen to be released as singles, and the artwork for the album and for every song was created by Tim Cantor, an artist from San Diego.
Dan´s Father was so impressed by Tim´s style of work after seeing it in his gallery, that he bought his book and passed it on to the band. And although Imagine Dragons continued to view other artists work, they decided that Tim Cantor´s art perfectly matched the sound of the album.

This album was released in various versions. The standard version included 13 songs, while the Deluxe Edition included 4 additional songs. The International Deluxe Edition also included Warriors. There was even a Super Deluxe Edition featuring Battle Cry, Monster and Who We Are. The band released an Asian Tour Edition too, featuring remixes of their released singles. Finally, there was also a Spotify Imagine Dragons Deluxe Edition with the addition of the Broiler Remix of Shots.

Promotion

- The band teamed up with the Hard Rock Cafe, and were granted the first full access ever to take control of Hard Rock Cafe's internal video system to celebrate the release of Smoke + Mirrors. This meant access to more than 20,000 screens, with 151 locations worldwide. On February 12, 2014, Imagine Dragons used this access to hand pick the videos shown. They also autographed a signature series of T-shirts to be hidden amongst the racks of various Rock Shops. The T-Shirts and pin sales went towards the bands Tyler Robinson Foundation. The cafe offered Imagine Dragons inspired drinks, such as Dragon Berry Daiquiri, Radioactive Lemonade and non-alcoholic Imagine Smoothie.

- Imagine Dragons posted on December 12, 2014, via social media about hidden clues to upcoming songs. There were 13 puzzle pieces of the artwork for the album. After being combined, the cover and album title were revealed.

- 200 prize winning fans were flown in on January 24, 2015, by the band to attend a special listening event at the P3 Studio Art Gallery in the Cosmopolitan of Las Vegas. There was also an art exhibition of Tim Cantors work for the album. The fans were allowed to listen to the full album through headphones while enjoying Tim Cantors art. Later, Imagine Dragons gave an Interview and performed live for their fans.

- Together with Target the band aired the first ever live commercial performance during the Grammy Awards. After building a huge stage just off the Strip in Las Vegas (Fremont Street, downtown), Imagine Dragons performed the song Shots, live. The four minute long performance on February 8, 2015, was recorded with more than 20 cameras from different angles, including helicopter shots. On the ground, 360 degree screens surrounded the audience, bathing them in light. Fans also wore illuminated LED bracelets. As they stood cheering around the stage, their arms became part of the stage design. Billboard estimated the commercial costs at about 8 million US dollars. Shots jumped from no. 99 to no. 26 on iTunes the next day.

- The album artwork for the Smoke + Mirrors album featured a set of numbers that provided specific coordinates to prizes hidden in the desert of Nevada. The prize included drumsticks, an autographed guitar, signed polaroid pictures and a masterpass for free concerts for the entire tour. As well as the treasure hunt, there were quite a lot of things hidden in the cover of the album artwork. Hidden letters (from their songs), hidden hints about their previous album, a hidden date and according to the band, so far, every riddle hasn't been solved.

- Thirty winners chosen by iHeartRadio, from cities all across the US, took part in a small promotional tour from February 20 until February 26, 2015. The band partnered with Southwest Airlines and flew the fans from coast to coast on the Destination Dragons Tour. The destinations were small clubs in Los Angeles, Provo, Las Vegas and Atlanta. It was a good preparation for the bands upcoming Smoke + Mirrors world tour. Imagine Dragons paid homage to the small clubs in which their career started. The performances took place at The Troubadour (Los Angeles, CA), Velour (Provo, UT), Vinyl (Las Vegas, NV) and Terminal West (Atlanta, Georgia). During their flight from Las Vegas to Atlanta, the fans enjoyed a special acoustic concert above the clouds, at 35,000 feet. This performance was called Live at 35.

- The band filmed a concert in Toronto, Ontario (Canada) on July 4, 2015, and was released as a concert DVD („Imagine Dragons: Smoke + Mirrors live") and showed for a limited time in select movie theaters.

- A hunt for a secret show was made for the release of Smoke + Mirrors. Fans had to follow hints, search for hidden letters and bring them into the right order to find out where a very special, private concert by Imagine Dragons was happening. The concert held at Clinton's Cafeteria in Los Angeles, on September 30, 2015, was sponsored by iHeartRadio. This „Destination Unknown Secret Show" was also broadcast live in Times Square in New York City.

Music videos

"I Bet My Life"

It took three days to shoot the four minute music video for the first released single of Smoke + Mirrors. The video is about a boy who was, while fighting another boy, sucked under water in a dam where he loses consciousness. He imagines suddenly being in a house, but is looking outside the windows, the whole world is under water. In his vision, he falls asleep and then wakes up finding himself in a sailboat. After a short trip, the boat is sailing towards a waterfall. After plummeting down the waterfall, he finds himself in a City, carried by a crowd of people. Suddenly, he's pulled away from the people and he awakens to realize, he has been saved from drowning by the boy, that he was fighting with.

"Gold"

This song was recorded by Dan at the beach, on the West Coast. During an interview with Billboard, Dan said that if you listen closely to the sample of him whistling into his laptop by the ocean, you can hear a wave that crashed while he was recording it.

The video is, compared to the other videos of the band, quite minimalistic. The band is performing the song in front of a lot of stage lights, which immerses the scenery in blue and golden light.

Fun fact.... There are rumors that Dan actually sings the words „nut sack" at one point in the song.

"Shots"

This video is a great homage to the paintings of Tim Cantor, who also did the artwork for the album and for all songs of Smoke + Mirrors. It´s like visiting a big gallery in which paintings and reality merge. At one point in the video, you can see an Imagine Dragons fan named Kevin making a guest appearance, he was the winner of a competition to join the band filming their music video, and during the shoot, the band asked him if he'd like to appear in the video. And he wasn't the only one that had a guest appearance in the video...

The band also released a 360 degree video, an acoustic version and two additional videos (Shots - Broiler Remix) for this song.

Tour

After performing a pre-tour show in Sydney, Australia in March 17, 2015, the official Smoke + Mirrors World Tour started on April 12, 2015, in Santiago, Chile. The tour included over 100 shows, leading the band to South America, Europe, North America, Asia, Oceania, North America once again and finishing in Europe on February 5, 2016, in Amsterdam, The Netherlands. Interesting fact: During the encore song, The Fall, a lot of leaves were falling from the ceiling.... Simply beautiful!

Fun fact: A handful of the leaves had a "winner" sticker on it, that if taken to the merch booth, would win you a random autographed prize! Some of which even included pranks to the bands management team!)

The band were accompanied on this album tour by Will Wells on guitar, keyboard and percussion. A driving, movable gallery with pictures by Tim Cantor followed the band to every tour stop, so that the fans could enjoy his artwork before the show.

Surprising facts

These tracks also received plenty of attention on Spotify...

    I´m So Sorry   Dream   Friction

Album track, **I´m So Sorry** has more streams than the released single, Shots, and has been used several times in movie trailers and tv series. For example, it featured in season 3 of Orange Is The New Black (Netflix original series, 2015), in the trailer for Legend (Film, 2015) and Jack Reacher: Never go Back (IMAX trailer for the film, 2016) A remixed version was also used for Kung Fu Panda 3 (animated martial arts film, 2016).

Dream received some attention when it was used by Omega for their advertisement for the Olympic games in Tokyo 2021.

The song **Friction** appears in the trailer for Mission Impossible - Fallout, and also made an appearance in the third and final season of the series Crossing Lines.

When you listen to **Hopeless Opus** backwards, you can hear „There is an anagram" at 1:24 min. According to Dan, this song is the cornerstone of Smoke + Mirrors´ faith crisis.

The song **Warriors**, which is featured in the trailer for the 2017 film Wonder Woman, got a Platinum certification in the US.

Platz promised to shave his beard if Smoke + Mirrors hits #1 on the Billboard 200 chart. Bye beard....

Additional releases

During the tour, the band released two more non-album singles: Roots and I Was Me (a charity song for the Syrian Refugee Crisis) via iTunes. To support the victims of the attacks in Paris, November 2015, Imagine Dragons also released a cover version of „I Love You All The Time" (by Eagles of Death Metal).

On June 30, 2015, the band collaborated with X Ambassadors. The song Fear, featuring Imagine Dragons, is the second single for X Ambassadors´ first studio album, VHS. It was produced by Imagine Dragons and Alex da Kid.

After their almost one year tour of Smoke + Mirrors, the band took a hiatus. By tweeting „goodnight +" on January 24, 2017, the band ended officially the era of Smoke + Mirrors. Before releasing their next album, the band worked on songs for various films like Me before you (Not Today), Suicide Squad (Sucker For Pain) and Passengers (Levitate).

From the second that I was born, it seems I had a loaded
gun
And then I shot, shot, shot a hole
Through everything I loved
Oh, I shot, shot, shot a hole
Through every single thing that I loved

Shots
Smoke + Mirrors

TIM

CANTOR

We´ve already mentioned in the chapter about the album Smoke + Mirrors that the artist, Tim Cantor was very involved in the making of the record. Not only did he create the album cover artwork, he even painted pictures for every single song on the album. A special exhibition was held where the fans could admire Mr. Cantors art while listening to the matching Imagine Dragons songs using headphones during DTS. The artist (and his art) even joined the band on parts of the Smoke + Mirrors Tour. You see, there´s a special bond between Imagine Dragons and Tim Cantor which is why we will give you more information about this fascinating artist.

Mr. Cantor was born on August 10, 1969, north of San Francisco. His father, an engineer, recognized his son's unique talent for drawing when Tim was only 5 years old. He gave him a box of oil paints and brushes that once belonged to Tims´ great grandfather. He instantly felt he had found his niche, creating paintings with oil and his obsession began. When Tim Cantor was only fifteen years old he was given the opportunity to have his first gallery exhibition at which one of his painting was acquired to hang in the White House.

Over the years, his paintings were displayed at exclusive exhibitions in Athens, Tokyo, Singapore, Paris, Venice, New York, Beverly Hills and San Francisco. Animals, portraits, trees, intricate fabrics are often mixed stylized scattered visions in his paintings. Interestingly, the letters of his beloved wife's name, Amy, often find their way into Tim´s work, hidden somewhere in his masterpieces.

He began working closely with Imagine Dragons by the end of 2014. Tim created the cover for their album Smoke + Mirrors, which reached number one in the world on the Billboard Top 200. Thirteen paintings which he created to represent every single song of the album as well as some of Mr. Cantor´s other masterpieces went on tour as a mobile gallery to accompany the band. His art was shown at over sixty shows throughout North America and Asia and his incredible stage design for the tour could be admired by fans worldwide.

And here are some interesting facts about Tim Cantor:

- He keeps far from the crowd, shrouded in his studio and works there every night from midnight until morning.

- Tim Cantor is fascinated, nearly obsessed with numbers and time.

- He likes to add elaborate technical devices, circles and strings in many of his artworks. He started adding these items around the age of thirty-five.

- Films based on the tales of H.G. Wells, Mary Shelly and also Jules Verne were Tim Cantor´s favorites as a child and he continues to likes this genre even as an adult.

- Painting isn't his only passion. He also writes beautiful and meaningful poems.

- He has completly self-taught himself by studying, interpreting techniques and applying his insight to his own distinct imagination.

- Tim´s art is also featured in the music video for Imagine Dragons single, Shots. He made a cameo in which he portrayed the character of the painting which he had created for the song I´m So Sorry.

- He travels to Venice every year to get perfect, unique frames specially created for his extraordinary paintings.

- In March 2021, Tim Cantor collaborated with Terra Virtua Ltd. the world's first fully immersive entertainment platform. Together, they took six of his traditional oil paintings and brought these incredible pieces to life, using animation techniques also known as NFT´s.

- Tim Cantor loves cats. He grew up with them. Tim and his wife, Amy's first cat was a grey and white female cat named Bean. Her spirit appeared periodically in Tim´s paintings. One year after Bean passed away at the age of 21 years, Tim and Amy adopted the Sphinx cat "Rapunzel".

- "The Selfless Ballerina", a painting which represents the song It Comes Back To You from Imagine Dragons´Album Smoke + Mirrors is one of the very few pieces that shows Tims beloved wife, Amy.

- "I usually have anywhere from 20 – 30 oil paintings that I am working on in my studio at any given time and it takes me just about two years to complete a collection of approximately 25 paintings. Each painting has about 50-100 layers of oil paint, glazes, and varnish along with all the tiny details that go into my work." Tim says in an interview with Terra Virtua.

- It is his passion to seek out and use the same materials (oil paint) and grind and mix the pigments just as artists did 500 years ago.

- A few famous collectors of his art are baseball player Bob Scanlan, Robert De Niro, Robert Redford, director Guillermo del Toro, and the band Imagine Dragons.

- He supports the charity organization TRF with his art which is sold in the TRF online store as t-shirts and other items. He also donated a few of his paintings for the auctions at TRF Galas. In 2019 Tim and Amy Cantor were honored by the organization by receiving the TRF Legacy Award.

To learn more about Tim Cantor and his art, please have a look at www.timcantor.com or visit his galleries, located in San Diego, USA and in Amsterdam, The Netherlands.

All I believe, is it a dream that comes crashing down on me?
All that I hope, is it just smoke and mirrors?
I wanna believe
But all that I know
Is it just smoke and mirrors?

Smoke And Mirrors
Smoke + Mirrors

Evolve

The Evolve era started on September 27, 2016, with just one simple tweet: „Studio". This amazing new album was released on June 23, 2017, by KIDinaKORNER and Interscope Records. It was partly recorded at the Ragged Insomnia Studios in Las Vegas, the band's very own studio. The artwork for this album was made by the artist Beeple (Mike Winkelmann). The band released four singles from Evolve: Believer, Thunder, Whatever It Takes and Next To Me.

The standard album was released with eleven tracks, and one more song as digital re-release (Next to me). A Deluxe Edition was also available with additional songs: Levitate, Not Today and a remix of Believer. The Japanese edition of Evolve had the song Roots added as a bonus track. The band had performed this song during the Smoke + Mirrors tour.

Promotion

- Promotion for „Evolve" started with a picture of Wayne in Imagine Dragons´ recording studio, which was tweeted by the band in September 2016. This tweet was followed by many other cryptic contributions on social media, all of which included the „ƎE" sign.

- To tease their first single, Believer, the band tweeted four videos. Vocalist Dan Reynolds was drawing surreal images in time-lapse videos. The band hid a morse code in the videos, which could be translated to „objects of same color".

- Imagine Dragons teamed up with Adobe and shot a few scenes for Believer from different angles and provided the material for a contest, so, the video could be edited by fans. The band and other experts in video editing then decided out of 9000 submitted videos which edit was the best. The video featured Dolph Lundgren and a perfectly sculptured Dan Reynolds.

- Pre-order of the album started in May 2017, along with the release of their single Whatever It Takes.

- The album cover artwork for Evolve provided two hidden codes for people to find. One led the fans to a location in the desert where several items of treasure were buried, one of which was a guitar that belonged to Wayne. The second code's prize was for two lucky fans to have a Meet and Greet with the guys, that was filmed by director Matt Eastin.

- On June 15, 2017, the band performed a show in Los Angeles using VR (Virtual Reality) so that fans had the feeling of being at the venue, watching Imagine Dragons live, in the comfort of their own homes using their VR equipment.

- Walking The Wire was available on June 15, 2017, as a free download with any purchase in Imagine Dragons online store.

- The song Roots was teased by the band changing their social media profile pictures to all black, with the caption „My Roots". Each member then started to post pictures of themselves as children, using #MYROOTS. The fans all followed suit, with the end result being a giant collage using all the pictures.

Music videos

"Believer"

In this video, Dan boxes against the actor Dolph Lundgren. It is assumed that Lundgren represents the future version of Dan. There are also a few scenes with a young boy, scribbling on a notepad. Both men are fighting hard, and at one point, Dan stops and says: I wanna stop" Dolph replies: „We can't". At the end of the video, the camera shows what the boy (played by Dan Reynolds's nephew, Max) was scribbling: .....The „Evolve" sign... „ƎE". We will leave the video to your interpretation.

To get in shape for this video, Dan took a month worth of boxing lessons and adhered to a strict keto diet regime designed by his personal trainer. Dan revealed in an Interview that whilst filming, Dolph accidentally caught him with a straight right to the jaw which almost knocked him out, and it´s said that the scene was actually used in the video.

Have you noticed the little He-Man figure lying next to the little boy on his chair? It´s an easter egg and a reference to Dolph Lundgren's former role in Masters Of The Universe. In August 2021, the video surpassed 2 billion views on YouTube.

"Thunder"

The video for the song Thunder was shot in Dubai and was filmed completely in black and white. Dan Reynolds is dancing and singing with extraterrestrials at popular areas like Shaikh Zayed Road, the City Walk and Dubai Marina.

During their stay in Dubai and filming the video, the band teased their fans with photos of themselves enjoying the desert. They also posted a pic of the famous Burj Khalifa to give a hint about their whereabouts. Dan came up with the Idea of shooting a video featuring extraterrestrials after he was accidentally punched by Dolph Lundgren on the set of the Believer video.

"Whatever It Takes"

In this video, the band performs the song as if on stage and not a single thing can discourage them... There's an earthquake? They continue to play. The room fills up with water? Not a problem. Everything is on fire, even their instruments, but still they don't stop.

It was shot in the O-Theater of the famous Bellagio Hotel in Las Vegas. For the underwater scenes, the band even did some scuba diving training. The set for the video shoot was inside the gigantic pool of the O Theatre, so that it was possible to dive, swim and float for the ultimate effect.

It´s amazing how many Easter Eggs are hidden in this video. It's full of innuendos to the band's other videos and songs. There are also references to people who made this video. Director Matt Eastin hid a picture of Corey Fox in it. Corey created the set and is also an old friend of the band. We will tell you more about Easter Eggs in a later chapter of this book.

The band provided also a 360 degree lyric video for this song.

"Next To Me"

This masterpiece is almost more of a film than a music video at nearly 12 minutes long. The story is devastating: A man (Dan) is having marriage problems, and his wife (Aja) leaves him. Consequently he tries to sell his wedding ring at a pawn shop. When he doesn't get the money he was hoping for, he loses control and in the heat of the moment, shoots the pawn shop owner (Wayne), which leads to him being arrested and then sentenced to death, but he gets the chance to see his wife one last time when released on parole. At this point of the video there are lots of flashbacks, which gives the film quite a mystical feel. Sadly, tragedy strikes with the video ending by Dan being executed by lethal injection.

It took four days to shoot the video at locations in Los Angeles and Las Vegas. Dan had to face his fear of confined spaces by shooting scenes in a tiny prison cell, his worst nightmare. This was filmed in a real, disused prison.

The video is packed full of metaphors and allusions, so there's a great scope for interpretation. The video director, Mark Pellington, explains in an interview: „The film is complex and slightly surreal fable about forgiveness and redemption. It is a story of a man and a projection of one fantasy colliding with the dark reality of fate. It asks, can a person who has made a terrible mistake be forgiven by their loved one or even by themselves."

"Roots"

The music video for Roots was shot in Auckland, during Imagine Dragons Smoke + Mirrors tour. When Dan realized, he was going to be in New Zealand, and that he'd have a day off, he called Matt Eastin, the director of the video, at 2am on a Monday morning and said he wanted to shoot a music video on Friday. When he was asked, about what he wanted the video to be like, Dan replied: "I don't know, let's figure something out!" Matt flew to New Zealand with his cinematographer, Ty Arnold, bought a „Red Dragons" 6K camera and shot the video with Dan. After 7 days of editing with only 10 hours of sleep for the director, the video was released on the same day as the song was launched.

„The video was very real," Eastin says. „We weren't telling Dan how to act. They were natural experiences that we just captured." The home videos of Dan as a kid are genuine, the director watched more than 20 hours of videos to find the snippets that made it into the final cut. Fun Fact: The underwater scene was filmed in the bathtub in Dan´s hotel room.

In the video, Dan is recovering from a very energy loaded concert. In his thoughts, he's wandering around, enjoying nature, getting in contact with people, and he has childhood flashbacks — his roots.

Tour

Starting in Phoenix, Arizona on September 26, 2017, the band performed about 140 shows in locations such as North America, Asia, Europe, South America and Oceania. The last show took place on November 18, 2018, in Mexico City.

During this tour, Imagine Dragons had a few surprises for the fans. On top of a shiny production of warm colors provided by the massive light structure, the band had fun with oversized balloons, bubbles, confetti and they even treated the fans that sat furthest away to a fantastic view on a second stage, set towards the back of the arena. The band were accompanied on this album tour by Eliot Schwartzman on keyboards, percussion, guitar and backing vocals.

Surprising facts

The Evolve album on Spotify also held a few surprises when it comes to album tracks that weren't released as singles. The following songs in particular, did well.

Walking The Wire   Rise Up   I Don´t Know Why

Walking The Wire was released as a promotional single and available for free download with every purchase on the band's online shop.

The lead single **Believer** featured in a commercial for Nintendo Switch Superbowl LI and in the trailer for the film Murder On The Orient Express (2017).

Thunder was recorded in a big room in Dan´s house in Las Vegas. Dan mentioned in various interviews, that he enjoys creating and recording in chaotic and noisy surroundings. During the recording of Thunder, you could hear Dan´s daughter, Arrow yelling in the background. Wayne tried to fix that when Dan sent him the song.

Additional releases

Before the band launched their 4th studio album, they released „Live at AllSaints Studios". This EP, released on August 3, 2017, featured Thunder, Believer, Whatever It Takes and Hand In My Pocket.

On December 15, 2017, Imagine Dragons released a **box set** consisting all of their albums on vinyl, starting with the Continued Silence EP, Night Visions (Standard Edition), Smoke + Mirrors (Super DeLuxe edition) and Evolve (Standard Edition).

In 2018, a **compilation** of the standard versions of all three Imagine Dragons albums: Night Visions, Smoke + Mirrors and Evolve was released in France.

„German Radio Live Sessions" was released on the same day as the band launched their next studio album. The EP featured songs taken from live performances on various German Radio Stations. The track list included Believer, It's Time, Mad World, On Top Of The World, Radioactive, Semi Charmed Life, Thunder, Whatever It Takes and I Bet My Life.

Matt Eastin

Matt Eastin followed and supported the band right from the beginning. He shot one of Imagine Dragons´ first videos on his camcorder. He directed several of their other incredibly creative music videos including On Top Of The World, Shots - Broiler Remix, Whatever It Takes and most recently Follow you, Cutthroat and Wrecked. Over the years they have developed a strong relationship built on trust. This close relationship is almost tangible in their collaborations. So, let's shine a light on this incredibly talented director.

He was born on June, 3rd 1979 in Fresno, California. He went to grade school there and also in Boardman, Ohio. Matt attended high school in Utah. At the age of nineteen he went on a 2 year church mission to Lima, Peru. While attending Utah Valley University (UVU), Matt had his first experiences with video in the media industry. He worked behind the camera to create content for the TVs around the campus hallways (although he confesses that he hates this now). Watching the editors in the newsroom piqued his interest in that side of the business, so he taught himself at first and then ended up taking some editing courses.

In 2004, he was hired straight out of university for his first job as a backup cameraman and editor for a travel show for Women's entertainment. Matt had tried a few other jobs in the industry but he wasn't passionate and enthusiastic about them. He discovered that making music videos was always his dream, so he quit his job and started his own film/production company, The Violet Suitcase. He started making free music videos for bands because Matt wanted to be known as „the music video guy" and one of his first projects was for a young band called Imagine Dragons.

During college, Matt met the love of his life, Shayla. He had to go through a great deal of effort to win her heart, because she was already engaged when he met her. But love always wins, so finally they got married and now the couple has three kids and they live a „picture perfect life" together in Utah.

And here are some interesting facts about Matt Eastin:

- Matt is bilingual. He speaks Spanish as a second language. This is a souvenir from his mission in Peru.

- He was studying journalism and broadcast communication at UVU.

- Audio-Files, a 14 episode lasting series featuring Imagine Dragons and other artists was directed and produced by him.

- He is very passionate about his career. He stays up all night working, because he wants every video to be great. He even did that for free music videos as investment in his own brand.

- In an Interview he confesses: „I feel like I'm an editor first and a director second. Because I know how to edit, it helps me when I'm on set directing. I'm not just getting a bunch of footage and then handing it to somebody else and saying, "All right, fix it." I have to live with my mistakes because I directed and then I always edit what I direct."

- Neon Trees, Aja Volkman, Pearl Jam and The Head and the Heart are just a few artists/bands he has worked with.

- Apart from documentary style series like Audio-Files and Studio C (he told us, he only made a rather small contribution to Studio C. He made a few of their opening credit sequences and a few of their music video sketches), Matt also created some commercials, but his passion is and will always be making music videos.

- It is more important to him to do a job he really likes than to earn a lot of money. He even drove a Honda with a cracked windshield because he always quit the jobs he hated.

- He's a member of The Occidental Saloon which is known by Imagine Dragons fans for having created the acoustic video for „It´s Time". The Occidental Saloon is a collective group of people whose intention it is to put raw, partly acoustic videos together.

- Matt was shooting (for fun) at the venue, when the band met Tyler Robinson at the club Velour in Utah for the first time. He witnessed the heartwarming scene when Dan sang It´s Time, together with Tyler. The rest, as they say, is history.

- He partnered with Adobe in the „Make The Cut" competition. Every participant received raw footage from „Believer" by Imagine Dragons and had a chance to win $25000 by editing the material and creating a unique video.

- Even after creating successful videos like Believer or On Top Of The World, he still occasionally makes music videos pro bono, first, because he loves it and second, it´s also a savvy marketing tool.

- He collaborated a lot with Corey Fox, the owner of the legendary club Velour in Provo, Utah. Corey co-directed On Top Of The World with Matt. He also did art direction for a few other videos (Cutthroat is one of them). Do you remember all these hidden easter eggs in Imagine Dragons´ videos? We have to credit Matt and Corey (and the band of course) for that!
Thank you, guys!

- Matt Eastin and his co-director Aaron Hymes´ video for Whatever It Takes won an MTV VMA (Video Music Award) for Best Rock Video in 2018.

- He also loves to work with Ty Arnold. He's Matt's DP (Director of Photography) for several of his videos. They both collaborated together for On Top Of The World, Believer, Roots and more recently the Follow You performance at the school and also the official Cutthroat video.

You can have a closer look at his work by following him on Instagram or Facebook.

Most days I´m keeping to myself
Living in my little bubble
Throwing my weight and
Moving my body through this sea
You could come join me

Dancing In The Dark
Evolve

Origins

On November 9, 2018, Origins was born. The band described the album as a sister album to Evolve and said that the two records would complete a circle of their music. Dan revealed in an Interview: „It's about seeking new ground, but also appreciating your roots. When we create, we create with no boundaries, no rules. We find it thrilling to make music that feels different and new to us."

Several items of merchandise and the Origins album cover was leaked online on October 2, 2018. The band officially announced the album to the public with a trailer, the next day. The cover for the Origins album was created by the artist Beeple.

There were five singles released from Origins: Natural, Zero, Machine, Bad Liar and Birds. The album consists of twelve songs. There was also a Deluxe edition that added Birds, Burn Out and Real Life and also an International Deluxe Edition that featured Born To Be Yours (with Kygo, track no. 16).

Promotion

• The Origins album launch on November 7, 2018, was a big deal for fans. There was a competition with the opportunity to win tickets for the show. The winners were picked up at the airport, enjoyed a full day in the company of Mac Reynolds (Imagine Dragons´s Manager and Dan´s brother) in Las Vegas and finally, they were part of a huge show to celebrate the launch of Origins. During the show, the band performed a selection of their hits from all albums and each band members also reminisced about their roots. Throughout the show, they gave awards to the people who have stood by their side right from the very beginning. A professor from Berklee college, a booking agent, a sound engineer and of course their families were amongst them. One of the many highlights was the performance of the song, Destinations, together with Brittany and Andrew Tolman... two of the former band members.

• The song Natural was chosen by ESPN as the anthem of the 2018 College Football season.

- The band kept the tradition of hiding things in the album artwork, just as they did with Smoke + Mirrors and Evolve albums. Apparently, only one riddle has been solved, and that was the song title of Hopeless Opus, hidden in mirror writing. We can only speculate, what else they wanted us to find.

Music videos

"Natural"

In a press release that announced this song Dan said: „It would be a lie to tell you I haven't become somewhat skeptical about some things in the last decade of my life. However, I believe that when you truly learn to love yourself, the judging eyes and hateful words become meaningless. „Natural" is about finding yourself and being willing and able to stand up to whatever adversity comes your way."

The video has a strong gothic horror feel to it. Dan is the owner of a dark and ghostly house, which is fallen into ruin. His outfit is from the American Civil War era, and he sits in a dining room which is covered in cobwebs, dust and insects. Suddenly, a character with very long arms appears - Slender Man. The piano starts playing all by itself, there are people dressed like ghosts or mummies, dancing. There's even a small horned goat (a depiction of the devil) amongst them. A beautiful girl drowns in the bathtub and Dan is seen digging a hole for her grave in the garden. While the girls funeral is taking place, he dreams of her running in the garden, wielding a knife.

There are people stood around the graveside, all dressed in black, who are also covered with dust, along with white, ghostly looking people in the garden, Slender man makes another appearance at this point, too. Dan clutches his hands to his chest, when he removes them, there's a hole right through him, as if his heart has been ripped out. After the girl is buried, Dan lays on her grave, desperately hitting the soil above her, with clenched fists, in disbelief that she is gone.

There was also a lyric video released, which is a little less spooky and has a completely different storyline.

"Zero"

This song showcases an Imagine Dragons speciality: An upbeat melody combined with darker lyrics. It was used in the Disney animated film „Ralph breaks the internet". At the release, Dan said: "Ralph's internal struggle for self-acceptance really resonated with us, and this song speaks to that."

In the official video, the band members star as employees and gamers in a 1980s style arcade. Singer Dan´s character has an oversized, Pacman-esque head, and the other members of the band characters are typical employees and arcade players. The video follows the characters at the arcade whilst doing their work and playing games.

There are also Disney Easter Eggs hidden in the original song video, but also watch the Imagine Dragons lyric video of this song! It's well worth it.

"Bad Liar"

The song was co-written by Dan Reynolds and his wife, Aja Volkman during a crises in their marriage. The video was shot at Green Valley High School, Nevada, and features a young couple in their school. The girl (played by Autumn Miller) is desperately and passionately dancing around her boyfriend, while he remains completely passive. He seems to be floating in the air, as if there were an invisible rope attaching him to the ceiling. The girl is fighting for their relationship, but as she gets no response from the boy, she decides to give up. As she leaves the building, the boy collapses and falls to the ground. But it´s too late, the girl has already gone.

Like most videos of Origins, this song was also released as a lyric video. Later, the band also launched a stripped back version of Bad Liar.

"Birds"

After releasing the single Birds, the band also launched a second version with the Italian singer Elisa.

In this animated video, a young girl inherits the power, from her Mother to change into a bird-version of herself and fly. She is bullied for this special power, and so keeps her identity hidden. She starts to hate her bird identity as her schoolmates laugh at her, due to her feathers and wings. As she grows up, pupils at school keep their distance, leaving her lonely and without friends. She hates herself so much that she even starts pulling her feathers out of her face. Sadly, her mother dies by sacrificing herself to save her daughter's life.

This song has emotional and meaningful lyrics that we all should pay attention to. Just because someone is different, they shouldn't be excluded by society. It also highlights the message that it's important to love and accept yourself, the way you are. Never change for someone else.

"Born To Be Yours"

It is a collaboration of Imagine Dragons and Norwegian music producer Kygo. The music video was directed by Matt Eastin, who also directed Roots, Shots Broiler Remix, Whatever It Takes, On Top Of The World Believer, Follow You and Cutthroat.

The video features a Sasquatch (or Bigfoot) on his quest to find love. After engaging with a female over social media and arranging a meeting, the Sasquatch is followed by hunters whilst on route to see her. When his truck breaks down, the hunters chase him off through the woods. When he finally reaches her house, he lets himself in to find numerous stuffed animal heads mounted on the walls, and suddenly realizes that the girl he was due to meet is also a hunter. Before he manages to make his escape, she captures him and chains him up beside a fellow Sasquatch that she had caught earlier.

He manages to free himself from the chains and rescues the other (female) Sasquatch. They fall in love with each other and the video ends with them riding on a motorbike together, off into the sunset.

A lyrics video for this song was also released by Kygo and Imagine Dragons.

Tour

To this day, Imagine Dragons have never toured with this album.

Surprising facts

The most streamed album tracks from Origins were:

West Coast   Boomerang   Cool Out

The song **Love** has been featured in a public service commercial by Pass It On.com, from The Foundation for a Better Life.

The song title **Real Life** was revealed during a live Twitter Q&A by Imagine Dragons and Dan said in an interview, it's one of his favorite songs of the album.

Additional releases

Imagine Dragons collaborated with the DJ Avicii for his Album „Tim". Sadly, Avicii passed away before its release. The song Heart Upon My Sleeve was released along with the full album on June 6, 2019.

In 2019, but only available in France, an **Imagine Dragons Compilation** of Night Visions, Smoke + Mirrors, Evolve and Origins was released. The compilation contains the standard versions of all the albums, except for Origins in which the International DeLuxe Edition was used.

In 2020, the Band released a **Limited Edition Album** of their hits Radioactive, Demons, Thunder and Bad Liar, all on 10" vinyl. This album is part of the „Runde Sache" (Round thing) charity campaign. It's a collaboration of Universal Music and the MediaMarkt/Saturn Group. Only 2020 records were created and it is only available at local shops. It should support the local record dealers, who are struggling due to the Covid-19 disease.

In the end of 2020, Imagine Dragons digitally released some old and previously unreleased songs on their official website. The page Deep Cuts contained an hour long backstage documentary about the bands Smoke + Mirrors album. And the following songs as audio files: All Eyes, All For You, Darkness, Destination, Emma, February, Lost Cause, Lovesong, Not Giving In, Pantomime, Stand By Me, Take My Heart Away and 30 Lives.

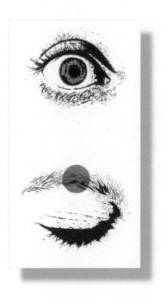

Beeple

Mike Winkelmann, better known by his alias, Beeple, created the cover artwork for Imagine Dragons Evolve and Origins albums. Not only was his art chosen for the two albums and their corresponding singles, but he was also the inspiration for the stage design of the Evolve tour. These are enough reasons to pay more attention to him..

Mr. Winkelmann was born on June, 20th, 1981 in Maiden, North Carolina and raised in North Fond du Lac, Wisconsin, USA. He graduated with a degree in Computer Science from Purdue University; however, he never received formal training in art. He began as a designer working on corporate websites, but as his graphic design skills improved, he started to work as a freelancer for various companies.

His speciality is digital artworks, including short films, virtual and augment reality (VR/AR) as well as Creative Commons VJ loops. Imagine Dragons were not his only famous clients. He also worked with artists like Justin Bieber, Katy Perry, Nicki Minaj, Eminem and One Direction. His work is also in great demand by popular companies like Apple, Space X, Nike, Coca-Cola, Adobe, Louis Vuitton and Samsung just to name a few. Lately, he was in the news because his NFT (**n**on-**f**ungible **t**oken) „Everyday: The First 5000 Days" sold for almost 70 million US dollars at an auction on Christie´s. The incredibly talented graphic designer currently lives in Charleston, South Carolina, USA.

And here are some interesting facts about
Mike Winkelmann:

- He has created a picture everyday and posted it online for nearly fourteen years without missing a single day. This extraordinary action is known as his „The Everyday Project".

- He doesn't consider himself a highly motivated, disciplined person.

- He tries hard not to read comments he receives from his followers or to look at how many likes his posts get, because he feels like feedback on the internet is not very helpful.

- He has been doing art since 2008.

- His advice for any artist that just getting started is „Don´t overthink. Making anything is always better than doing nothing".

- Mike Winkelmann named himself Beeple after a 1980s furry toy. It´s nose lit up in response to sound and light.

- He has no gallery representation or any other foothold in the traditional art world.

- Almost 2 million Instagram followers are enjoying his art.

- Although he is very successful with selling his art, he can't quite shake the feeling that without some physical object to go along with the NFT, he was kinda maybe only selling „magic beans".

- When asked about his biggest influence, he said that he was influenced by some films, but especially Star Wars was inspiring.

To see more of his art, please visit:
https://www.beeple-crap.com

Mercury Act 1

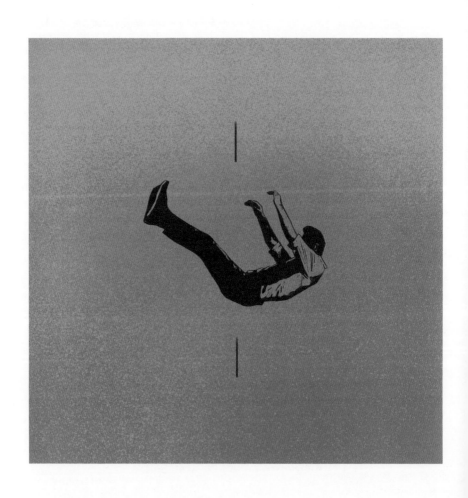

Mercury Act 1 & 2

Part one of Imagine Dragons album Mercury was released on September 3, 2021. The band chose 4 singles to represent the album. Cutthroat and Follow You were launched together, and about 3 months later, Wrecked and Monday were released.

The promotion of Mercury Act 1 started in spring 2021. The cover art of the first two singles illustrate the concept of the complete album pretty well. One closed eye implies the sight to the inner part of oneself, whereas the opened eye shows how the world perceives you (or: the way, you see the world).

Although a lot of people think that the album name is related to the roman god Mercury, Dan explains the album title in an interview differently: The album title actually comes from the word: mercurial. It means something that is very volatile, subjective, extreme changes. „That's me in a nutshell" Dan said. „My entire life has been pretty bipolar. And so is my music. Sometimes I want to write a really angry rock song, and sometimes I want to write a pretty soft pop song. The whole album pretty much swings from side to side."

Imagine Dragons worked with the famous producer, Rick Rubin to complete this album. The cover art was created by a London based agency. Mat Maitland, Creative Director at Big Active, did the beautiful artwork for Follow You, Cutthroat, Wrecked and the album cover for Mercury Act 1. Mr. Maitland has worked with Michael Jackson, Kenho, Louis Vuitton, Hermes, Apple,...

In an interview, Dan said that he recorded the song, Follow You, in his own house and not in Rick Ruben's recording studio (Shangri La in Malibu). Dan said he just didn't get the right feeling in California, so they used the version previously recorded on Dan´s laptop for the album.

When asked what this record is about, Dan says, „It is about honesty and facing the finality of life and what this feels like. Sometimes it´s scary, sometimes it´s beautiful, sometimes it´s confusing." Rick Rubin pushed Dan and the band to uncomfortable places. After Dan had him to listen to some demos, Rick just told him, „I don´t believe you", and this simple statement led Dan to finally create a very vulnerable record.

In April 2022, the band announced the release date (July 1, 2022) of Mercury Act 1 & 2, but it wasn't a great surprise to the fans anymore. An over-enthusiastic journalist had leaked the date about 6 hours earlier.

"Bones" and "Sharks" were chosen by the band to represent the album as singles. "Bones" was used for the Amazon exclusive series „The Boys". The album's second single, "Sharks", was published only a few days before the album release. Imagine Dragons dropped the music video for Sharks just a few hours later.

Dan Reynolds let fans know in an interview, that Mercury Act 1 and Act 2 are about dealing with death. Act 2 is more focused on the things that happen after death, after grief, when life goes on, and you have no choice but to continue living. But after you have lost someone, you realize, that every moment counts, as tomorrow isn't guaranteed for anyone. „´Cause this breath could fade fast and this day could be your last". (from „Waves")

On June 2, 2022, the band let their newsletter subscribers know about the track list for Mercury Act 2 first, and then few hours later, the band announced it on social media. They posted a short video slideshow with the song titles of their upcoming album.

Dan Reynolds explained the cover art for their albums during a question and answer session in Vienna: The cover art of Mercury Act 1 & 2 continues the circle that started with Night Visions. A little boy was standing on elevated stones and he was scared of the world. Dan said that the world felt like this for the band when they released their first studio album. That boy accompanied the band through the years and grew up in their five albums. The cover art of Mercury portrays an adult man that falls and rises. A metaphor for the ups and downs in life.

The band collaborated with Cory Henry for the song „Continual". Rick Rubin, the album's producer, came up with this idea. He wanted to follow in a gospel tinged direction and brought in Cory. He had worked with the band before, for Mercury Act 1 (Follow You and Cutthroat).

Imagine Dragons released a different version in Japan. It features versions of Believer (acoustic), Follow You (acoustic) , Wrecked (Live From The Bunker), Enemy (with Dan rapping) and Bones (Live From The Climate Pledge Arena). The song „I Wish" is also included in this edition.

Promotion

- The band sent 4 different videos to their fans worldwide. Each video contained short sequences of animals, there were hints about astrology, short snippets of songs... it was a chaotic mess. On top of that, there were also many messages hidden, which unveiled the date for the launch of the first two singles (Follow You and Cutthroat) and there was also a hint for the album title.

- Imagine Dragons made a cover contest on YouTube. Everyone could submit an own version either of Follow You or Cutthroat. The winner received $20.000 and a zoom video call from the band. A few weeks later, they did something similar to Wrecked, but the first place was awarded with $50.000.

- At „The Late Show with Stephen Colbert", the band played Follow You as a quite intimate studio performance. Imagine Dragons were also guests on „The Ellen DeGeneres Show" and performed Follow You with children from a school in Las Vegas singing backup. At Walmart's „Homecoming Concerts", ID performed at Dan´s alma mater, Bonanza High School, for free.

- To promote Follow You, Imagine Dragons released a jump and run game along with a matching video. The player had to chose a character (a member of the band) and try to catch as many diamonds as possible within the length of the song Follow you. Each level was happening on different planets, which represented the previous ID albums. At the end of each level, there was a big fight against a fire-breathing dragon.

- On July 30, 2021, the band tweeted a photo, saying "If anyone guesses the album title tonight, we will announce it tomorrow". Of course there was a hint for the album name hidden in that tweet. After changing the contrast of the picture, the letters revealed an anagram of „Mercury", the album name. An interesting detail, the band tweeted that on a Wednesday, „Mercredi" in French.

- A new section appeared on August 21, 2021, on ID´s website. To enjoy #MercuryAscending, a password is required. Two randomly chosen people, who solved the hints about this password, received tickets for every show of the Mercury World Tour and $2000 from Imagine Dragons. Another six people from different parts of the world received guitars signed by the band as a prize.

- Imagine Dragons started to promote the double album Mercury Act 1 and Act 2 while touring. There were rumors about a new song for the Amazon series „The Boys" because the band retweeted a poster for the new season. A few hours later, on the same day, March 10, 2022, Imagine Dragons announced Bones with a 13 sec video on the bands Discord server. They posted a video with Dan performing a very short version of the song only a few minutes later on TikTok.

- Bones has been used in a promotional video for a soccer match (Roma - Atalanta) in the Europe League.

- A special edition of Mercury Act 1 and Act 2 including an additional, new track (I Wish) is available at Target.

- The band released a teaser video with a short clip of a song from Act 2 on social media on June 14, 2022. This video contained a combination of letters, which told the fans, which song would be the second single of the album.

- Only a few days later, the band used Twitter and Instagram to tease their fans with a very special post. After they had sent puzzle pieces via email to their fans, Imagine Dragons posted a few hints about how to handle them on social media. Each puzzle piece contained a hidden code (binary, braille, morse and other methods). These clues led to 9 links. After the fandom put them in the correct order, it revealed a 30 second long teaser for Sharks, the second single from Act 2.

- Two days before the release of Sharks, the band announced on their social media platforms a special event. It was only available for residents of Austria, Germany or Switzerland. If you were one of 600 lucky people chosen, you were invited to an exclusive viewing of the music video premiere of Sharks in a cinema in Vienna. After having the amazing opportunity to watch Sharks, as well as the Bones video on the big screen, the fans were the first to listen to Mercury Act 2 - a week before its release. The album was played in the cinema while the lyrics to the songs were shown on the screen. But the event wasn't finished yet! For the last part, the internet community joined the audience at the Gartenbaukino. The band sat in front of the fans and answered their questions. The entire session was live-streamed on Instagram. The lucky fans got a very special gift after the event: a black cotton tote bag with an open and a closed golden eye and 2 exclusive posters of Sharks.

- Three days before the album was released, the band posted a short documentary about the making of the album with concert clips, snippets from their recent music videos and background songs from Mercury Act 2 (Younger, Sharks, Symphony, Bones). This promotional clip was directed by Matt Eastin (On Top Of The World, Whatever It Takes, Roots, Cutthroat, Wrecked,...).

- Although touring through Europe, Imagine Dragons did two promotional events on the release day of Mercury Act 1 & 2: They did an one hour long question & answer session with fans on Twitter (#AskDragons). Then, just two hours later a listening party with track breakdowns took place on the band's channel on Discord on July 1, 2022.

Image from Arcane, the Netflix series that „Enemy" was used as Title track for.

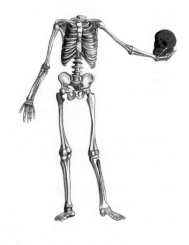

This picture symbolizes Bones, the first single from Mercury Act 2.

Music videos

"Follow You"

Follow You was released on March 12, 2021. Dan talked about the background of the song in various interviews. He and his wife, Aja, had a marriage crisis und due to his busy tour schedule, they hadn't been able to sort it out, and hadn't even talked in 7 months! When Dan was back home, they were going to meet for the first time again, but only to sign the divorce papers. Dan received a text message from Aja as he was on the way to the appointment at the lawyer's office. It basically said that Aja doesn't have to „own" Dan to love him. She was willing to let him go, but she also said, she will always love him. After arriving at the meeting, Dan looked at Aja and asked „Why are we getting divorced?" She just smiled and it ended up with them having lunch together, without having signed the papers. They celebrated their 10th wedding anniversary in 2021 and had another baby boy just one year after their „almost-divorce".

First, the band released a lyric video, and soon after that, they put out a surprisingly funny official video. Aja Volkman came up with the idea and it was directed by Matt Eastin. Rob McElhenney and his wife, Kaitlin Olson play a couple who are celebrating his birthday. Kaitlin has a pretty awesome surprise for her husband, an exclusive concert featuring his favorite band. His bad luck, she hired Imagine Dragons, her favorite band. During the band's performance, the couple is daydreaming. Kaitlin visualizes the members of ID, shirtless. Rob imagines himself performing shirtless with the band. In the end, they both realize that they already have their dream partner and there´s no need to fantasize about someone else. They leave the venue after only one song — which leaves Dan and the band baffled and unpaid.

The video was filmed at the Venetian in Las Vegas at the old Phantom of the Opera theater.

"Cutthroat"

Same as with Follow You, Imagine Dragons decided to release a lyric video for the song first. About one month afterwards, the band launched the highly anticipated, official music video.

Cutthroat is about eliminating this dark side of you that keeps telling you that you're not good enough, that causes anger and unhappiness and leaves you with self doubt. Try to get rid of this voice in your head! According to Dan Reynolds, this song is „An exorcism in self-pity."

Matt Eastin directed the video that shows Olivia Munn, just trying to get her driver's license. The actor, Adrian Martinez plays the driving instructor who put her under great pressure. During the driving test, he enjoys his tomato soup next to her. While she drives, he suddenly screams as he finds an insect in his lunch. She got frightened, makes a mistake and he immediately gives her a bad rating on her driving skills. This is the moment, when everything is getting too much for her. Overwhelmed by her feelings, she drives full speed and then stops and throws the driving instructor out of the car, right in the middle of nowhere. Back at the DMV (Department of Motor Vehicles), just before she can set the whole office on fire in her anger, her number is called and she finally receives her driver's license.

Don´t forget to look out for hidden Easter eggs (References to other ID songs) in this video! Interesting fact: Matt Eastin himself did a stunt in the video. The director drove the car while crashing into a gate and also almost ran over Mac Reynolds (He made a cameo as construction worker).

A few weeks later, ID released a „Cutthroat live" video, which was shot on the same location as the official music video and was directed by Matt Eastin as well. Also have a look at the awesome Behind the scenes video!

"Wrecked"

Released on July 2, 2021, this song was self produced and has a very personal and dark background. Dan spoke in several interviews about his sister-in-law, Alisha. She supported him and stood by his side during his marriage crisis with Aja. Throughout her life, she always emitted positive energy and a happy mood. Devastatingly, she got sick and was diagnosed with cancer. Only one year after the diagnosis, Alisha passed away. Dan was with her when she took her last breath in a clinic in Texas. This experience affected him deeply. After the release of Wrecked, he posted a tweet and a video, which showed the special bond between them. Dan said that Wrecked was written right after she passed away in 2019. A few days later, Dan also shared a few very personal pictures of Alisha.

Director Matt Eastin and director of photography, Ty Arnold were in charge of the official video for Wrecked. The video shoot took 3 days and happened in Miami and at the Cesars Palace Hotel in Las Vegas. The video shows the story of Dan and Alisha. He's featured in various daily situations like at a party, driving his car or taking a walk on the beach. He has Alisha in his mind in all these situations. She appears regularly in the background... always present, but never reachable for him. The video also provides a glimmer of hope, that our already passed loved ones are with us, giving us support and comfort.
What a beautiful thought.

Actress Jetta Juriansz, who plays Alisha, wears a yellow dress in the video. This is a tribute to Alisha, because according to her high school friend, she loved to wear that dress. The very last scene of the video shows Alisha Durtschi Reynolds and her family. In the background, you can hear her say: „When trials come, things that are important become really clear."

The band also released a lyric video for the song on the day of the release as well as a Making Of a few days later.

"Monday"

The band released the music video for „Monday", the fourth single from „Mercury Act 1", on September 24, 2021. Complementing the happy vibes of the song, the video is a real mood booster. Dan says about this song: "I love the cheekiness of it. Every time I listen to (the song), I smile."

The video is filmed in a retro-style house and documents the daily life of the band. Starting with preparing breakfast, later a bit of mini golf and relaxing at the pool, the guys seem to enjoy and love their life, if only there weren't the explosions and the loss of power... Just a few moments later, the secret is revealed: The band lives underground, in a bunker. The earth is facing many catastrophes (meteors, earthquakes, UFO attacks) and the end of the world is foretold by a newspaper.

On his Instagram account, Director Matt Eastin revealed how he came up with the idea for this creative video. One day, he saw a post of a real underground house in Las Vegas. He fell in love with the style of the building and after just a few short adjustments, the location was ready for the shooting of the „Monday" music video.

Of course, Matt couldn't resist adding a few Easter eggs. Some examples are the mention of „Ragged Insomnia" (Anagram for Imagine Dragons), the playing cards and dice referring to the band's hometown, Las Vegas (he previously used this reference in the video for Whatever It Takes). Additional Easter eggs include reference to the „Snogard Conspiracy" (this term was used in the On Top Of The World video), the song Thunder was mentioned and Matt Eastin himself had „written" an article for the newspaper shown at the end of the video.

A post on Facebook by Corey Fox (Art Director and in charge of wardrobe and props) showed that the crew obviously had fun shooting this video: „It was fun to be on a shoot where the smiling and laughing didn't end when the director yelled cut!".

As there is for all of the songs on „Mercury Act 1" there is also a lyric video for „Monday" available on the band's official YouTube channel.

"Bones"

The music video for Bones was released on April 6, 2022. After 6 days of preparation, shooting the video was a one day event. Director, Jason Koenig (who previously worked with Ed Sheeran, Elton John, Shawn Mendes,..), Choreographer, Alexander Chung and Make-up Artist Ally McGillicuddy raised the dead in this homage to Michael Jackson´s „Thriller".

Dan Reynolds is almost unrecognizable in this music video. He plays a day trader who is very successful in his job. After a great deal, he likes to celebrate with a very special dance in front of his colleagues. But, things get tricky when his co-workers suddenly turn into hungry zombies....

The Imagine Dragons frontman, said in an interview that he liked the idea of punishing Wall Street with a zombie infection. „Thriller", the spooky 1983 music video, is one of Dan Reynolds´ children's favorites. "I've always loved that "Thriller" is both scary and playful. I didn't know as a kid if I wanted to watch it again or not for fear of the ensuing nightmares, but I always came back for more with my eyes half-closed" says Dan.

You can find a very entertaining „Behind The Scenes"-video for Bones on YouTube. Enjoy the transformation of Wayne into a Zombie and witness Dan learning his choreography. The band also provided a lyric video for Bones.

In an interview with iHeart Radio, Dan says, "'Bones' is a reflection of my constant obsession with the finality and fragility of life, I'm always in search of some evidence that will convince me that there is more to come — that life is truly eternal in some sense. Having yet to find that, I try to at least dream of what conquering death would feel like in a song."

"Sharks"

The band was touring with Mercury Act 1 in Europe, when they dropped "Sharks". According to a snippet of the music video which was posted by the band a week before the release, the fans assumed that it was kind of a "James-Bond" or "Oceans Eleven" style video.

And they were right. Imagine Dragons´ frontman Dan Reynolds and his bandmates are working together with tricks and diversionary maneuvers to reach their goal. Dan has to overcome security guards, laser rays and other problems to finally get to a cordoned off room inside the Bellagio hotel. His mission was to free the sharks from the tank and to release them into the famous pool of the hotel. And he did it!! To celebrated his success, he surfed between these dangerous animals, with the famous fountains behind him.

Dan Reynolds said that it took him about 1 1/2 hours to learn to surf on the electric surfboard in the Bellagio fountains. Even though a stuntman was on the set, Dan wanted to do the stunt himself. This made a few fans very happy who were surprised to see the singer on a surfboard, followed by a camera drone.

This incredible video was directed by Drew Kirsch. He has worked with Taylor Swift, John Legend, Niall Horan and Shakira just to name a few. Sharks was filmed mostly at the Bellagio, Mandalay Bay and the Allegiant Stadium in Las Vegas. The shooting was done in 3 days in May 2022.

An interesting fact about the video: The shark tank is not in the Bellagio hotel, these amazing animals can be seen at Mandalay Bay´s aquarium in Las Vegas.

The lyric video for this song was released on July 14 on international Shark-awareness-day. There is also a behind-the-scenes video available on the band's YouTube channel.

Tour

Dan mentioned that the tour for Mercury will be the biggest tour they've ever done. In July 2021, the band announced the first dates for performances at festivals like the Openér Festival (Poland), NOS Alive (Portugal) and Lollapalooza (Paris).

Early September 2021, the band announced the tour dates for the North American leg of Imagine Dragons´ world tour. The tour started in Florida on February 6, 2022, and includes several shows across the United States Of America and Canada. Grandson Macklemore, Kings Elliot and MØ were the openers on the American leg, while Aviv supported them in Canada.

It is also possible to purchase special VIP packages for the tour that include early entry to the venue, merchandise gifts and autographed posters of the band to name just a few of the perks. A portion of all VIP package proceeds go directly to support the bands charity organization TRF.

The band announced the dates for the European leg of the Mercury Act 1 world tour on November 1. On their schedule are big cities like Berlin, Prague, Madrid and Paris, but the band performs also at smaller venues and at various festivals.

At an Imagine Dragons concert, you will find video sequences interwoven between the live music. Dan uses the full length of the stage with his high-energy performance. Similar to the Evolve tour, the narrator of the video sequences is former BBC newscaster John Cavanagh. He is also the narrator of Mr. Tim Cantor´s videos on his YouTube channel. The poems were written by Wayne Sermon. Wayne also had the idea of the Polaroid/ Hopeless Opus mashup. Elliot Schwartzman supports the band with keyboards, percussion, guitar and backing vocals.

Imagine Dragons love to surprise the fans and they are also very creative guys, so every band member designed their own piece of confetti for the tour. These unique scraps of paper fell on fans during the performance of The Fall at the North American leg of the tour.

The visuals and 3D animations on this tour were created by Lightborne and Polymath. Lightborne is an award winning company which also worked with AJR, Zac Brown Band, Billy Joel, and many more. Polymath is a small company made up of just 4 employees which focuses on advertising.

Surprising Facts

<u>Mercury Act 1</u>:

Cutthroat was originally started by Platz. He created the drum and guitar part, the backbone of this powerful song.

At the charity livestream in August 2021, Dan mentioned that his favorite song from this album is **My Life**.

For „Mercury Act 1", all songs needed to pass the „Rick Rubin guitar and vocal test" to make it on the record. Producer, Rick Rubin made the band play every song with an acoustic guitar. Either it sounded good or suddenly it didn't sound good anymore and so it didn't make it on the record. That was a pretty easy and effective way to choose the best songs for the album.

Monday, Giants and **It´s Okay** were co-written and co-produced by „Goldwiing". Behind this name hides non-other than founder band member Andrew Tolman and Wayne Sermon.

<u>Mercury Act 1 & 2</u>:

Tied was the first song that Dan wrote after he moved back in with Aja after their separation.

The first single of Mercury Act 2, **Bones**, was used for the Amazon series „The Boys", but is wasn't composed for that purpose, it was written before and just gained popularity because it was used for The Boys.

Wayne said on Twitter that **Take It Easy** is his favorite song. He also said that it was created in Platz´s studio "Platzcaster"

Dan got emotional about the song **Waves** during an Instagram Live Q&A. The song is about Dan´s best friend during middle school who took his life. Dan dedicated They Don´t Know You Like I Do to him as well.

According to one of his tweets, **Crushed** is very special to Platz.

Additional releases

On August 18, 2021, the band released a single called **Imagine Dragons** under the name Ragged Insomnia, which is an anagram for Imagine Dragons.

On October 22, 2021, Imagine Dragons shared the **TELYKast Remix of Demons**. This song was the second single from their 2012 album, Night Visions.

The band released their old EP´s officially for purchase and on various streaming platforms in Oct 2021. In addition to the original track list, the band added one bonus song to each album. **Imagine Dragons EP** featured Hole Inside Our Chests. Dan wanted to describe complete loss of faith without saying it out loud and it was the first demo, Wayne had heard from Dan. The song, Easy can be found on **Hell And Silence** and was Dan´s attempt to get himself to slow down and to stop self-hatred. It was created during the Smoke + Mirrors era. On **It´s Time**, the additional song is Dolphins. According to Dan, it was a song searching for serenity. It was written during the creation process for Night Visions.

On February 4, 2022, the band released a different version of Mercury Act 1 with an additional song as the first track. Imagine Dragons and the famous rapper JID (Destin Choice Route) partnered with RIOT Games and released the song „**Enemy**" for Arcane. Exclusively created for Netflix, this animated series is based on the video game League of Legends. The band also published a beautiful animated music video for the song which also includes characters from „Arcane" such as Vi and Jinx. The animation was done by Fortiche Productions, a french company from Paris and RIOT games was responsible for development and production of the series. It is the second time, that Imagine Dragons cooperated with RIOT Games. They already have collaborated very successfully together for the World Championship of League of Legends and created the song Warriors for this event in 2014. There was also a radio edit of Enemy which was released in November 2021. In this version, Dan did the rap part with different lyrics.

A few days after the release of Mercury Act 1 & 2, the band took Mercury Act 1 down from some music platforms (The original version with My Life as opening song and also the new edit with Enemy as first song) because all tracks from Mercury Act 1 are included in Mercury Act 1 & 2.

Rick Rubin

For their fifth studio album, Imagine Dragons reached out to legendary producer, Rick Rubin. Just in case, you're not familiar with him:

Frederick Jay Rubin (* March 10, 1963) was born and raised in Lido Beach (Long Beach), New York, USA. He had his first musical experiences playing in a band with his childhood friends. Later, he was part of a punk band called The Pricks. The biggest step into his music career was in 1984 when he, along with Russell Simmons at the University of New York, founded Def Jam Recordings.

He was only twenty-one when he started the company. Mr. Rubin once said that he doesn't care about musical genres, as long as the music is meaningful to him. Since he doesn't mind if it´s hip hop, country or rap, it´s no surprise that artists like LL Cool J, Run DMC and the Beastie Boys are signed to Def Jam Recordings.

Russell Simmons and Frederick Rubin split in 1988 and Mr. Rubin founded his own label Def American Recordings. In 1993, he changed the name to American Recordings. The list of the artists who worked with Mr. Rubin sounds like the who's who in the music industry, Public Enemy, Red Hot Chili Peppers, AC/DC, The Cult, System Of A Down, Tom Petty, Johnny Cash,.. The list is just endless.

2007 was a very successful year for him. Not only did he become co-President of Columbia Records alongside Steve Barnett, but also received a Grammy and was named in a poll in Time Magazine as one of the 100 Most Influential People In The World.

Mr. Rubin purchased the legendary recording studio, Shangri-La, in Malibu in 2011. The pay-TV channel Showtime even aired a four part documentary series about Shangri-La and its famous owner. Mr. Rubin left Columbia Records in 2012 and revived his American Recordings imprint as an arm of Republic Records which is a part of the Universal Music Group. In the year 2014, Frederick Ruben legally changed his name to Rick Rubin. A few years later, Imagine Dragons reached out to him to create a legendary album together...

And here are some interesting facts about Rick Rubin:

- In his musical career as producer he has been nominated 18 times for a Grammy award and won 9 of the trophies between 1997 - 2020.

- He produced the first crossover rap hit in the US in 1986. In collaboration with Run DMC, Aerosmith released a remake of their 1977 hit Walk This Way.

- Mr. Rubin practices Yoga and Zen meditation regularly.

- He finds new, interesting music online, mostly on SoundCloud.

- When Rick Rubin changed the name of his label and dropped the „Def" from Def American Recordings, he held a funeral at Hollywood Memorial Park Cemetery. Approximately 500 mourners attended this event amongst them, Trent Reznor of Nine Inch Nails, Flea of the Red Hot Chili Peppers and Tom Petty.

- „I don´t know what makes someone hip. The goal is artist achievement and best work we can do with no limitation" is one of his most famous quotes.

- He normally keeps weekends free for reading, walking on the beach, watching old movies and listening to music — but never his own. He also loves to hang out with his friends, such as Chris Rock and Director Wes Anderson.

Can you spot all the released singles?
And maybe something else.....

N	E	X	T	T	O	M	E	U	O	Y	W	O	L	L	O	F
D	W	C	O	D	E	K	C	E	R	W	S	H	A	R	K	S
L	N	H	R	G	A	R	H	V	F	U	N	G	B	S	E	Z
R	S	W	A	E	I	N	E	O	S	N	O	M	E	D	V	T
O	M	L	I	T	B	L	A	L	D	L	X	O	L	R	I	A
W	O	S	L	S	E	N	R	V	D	E	R	N	I	I	T	L
E	K	N	D	R	T	V	M	E	L	Y	E	D	E	B	C	P
H	E	I	A	O	M	E	E	A	U	D	D	A	V	Y	A	C
T	G	G	B	R	Y	N	N	R	D	M	N	Y	E	R	O	U
F	U	I	O	R	L	I	I	L	I	A	U	E	R	U	I	T
O	I	R	N	I	I	H	T	C	O	T	H	N	E	C	D	T
P	T	O	E	M	F	C	S	O	S	V	T	Y	M	R	A	H
O	A	Z	S	A	E	A	A	E	H	J	E	A	O	E	R	R
T	R	I	E	A	J	M	E	T	O	M	P	W	K	M	O	O
N	E	B	N	R	O	A	N	A	T	U	R	A	L	E	F	A
O	S	S	A	B	O	Y	I	T	S	T	I	M	E	O	S	T
S	N	O	I	S	I	V	T	H	G	I	N	S	M	U	R	D

I found these words:

_____

_____

_____

_____

_____

_____

_____

_____

_____

_____

_____

Little Known Facts About Imagine Dragons

Their first international gig was in Norway, at Bergen-Fest. This appearance was the top prize in a contest that they had entered. So they performed at this festival as a small, unknown band.

The band say that one of their worst performances was performing in a mall. They opened for the junior varsity cheerleader team at 9am... there was nobody there and they played so loudly that they were given disapproving looks and shops even closed their doors.

They once had a fan that came backstage and pretended to be a massage therapist, she even managed to get one of the band members half naked! (It was Platz.. 😶)

Semi-Charmed Life by Third Eye Blind was the first song that Imagine Dragons ever played together as a band.

Radioactive was chosen by the fans to be the bands second single from Night Visions. The decision was made after Radio stations were swamped with calls asking them to play the song, and therefor receiving a huge amount of attention.

On Top Of The World was performed by a children choir at the presidential inauguration of Barack Obama.

According to Platz, Wayne was once given an electric shock from his guitar.

Dan Reynold writes many of his songs using cryptic messages. The song Radioactive isn't as many people assume, about radioactivity, but is in fact about depression. Dan didn't want to worry his Mom, so he hid the true meaning of the song, by using a metaphor.

The band opened for American Idol darling Kelly Clarkson when she played in Salt Lake City.

When Dan founded the band, he called it Lavender, but the name was changed to Imagine Dragons soon after.

This is how the band spent their first big paychecks:
Dan bought a 1967´Mustang, Ben got a Toyota Tacoma, Platz sleeps now on a Tempur-pedic mattress and Wayne? He got a Japanese toilet!

They bought an old, weird '70s house outside of Las Vegas and turned in into their studio. The neighborhood had a reputation as being a rough area, and there were a lot of shady people, including drugs dealers. The album Smoke + Mirrors was recorded there. And to help them feel more comfortable, they decorated it with vintage gear and had a framed note from Sir Paul McCartney displayed on the mantelpiece.

Imagine Dragons had a gig, opening for the band Temper Trap. But Ben was in jail, apparently for a „series of bad choices", although Dan thinks it was probably for running around a hotel, naked. Twenty minutes before the show was due to start, Dan convinced the detention officer to let him out of jail early. She agreed to let Ben go after Dan offered her a signed CD from the band. Ben performed the gig in clothes he was wearing in the prison. „He was dismissed of all charges" Wayne said later in an interview.

The band provided a lot of songs for soundtracks to various sports games such as: FIFA 13, NBA 2K16, NBA 2K17, NHL, Pro Evolution soccer 13,... and their songs also featured in Rock Band 4, Guitar Hero Live and Battlefield Hardline to name just a few.

Platz was stalked for a few weeks, by a girl that he gave his phone number to. Weeks later, after the phone calls from the girl had stopped, his band members would call him, pretending to be her by breathing heavily down the phone whenever he picked up. This prank lasted for a whole year and Platz was extremely anxious about it, so her picture was put up everywhere at venues wherever the band performed. One day, the girl arrived to attend a concert and the police, recognizing her from the pictures, nearly arrested her. Dan then had to explain to the police, what was going on and revealed that they had been pranking Platz with the phone calls.

While still in college, Dan asked Corey Fox, the owner of the Velour in Utah, for a gig at his venue. Corey recommended that Dan should participate in the Battle Of The Bands competition first, which he did and won. That was the moment when Dan realized that he just has to make music. The rest is history.

Many people misheard the lyrics from Demons „where my demons hide" as „where Matt Damon hides". This misinterpretation became so popular that even the wifi hotspot from the ID crew members backstage is called „where Matt Damon hides".

They participated in a popular show called Impractical Jokers.

In 2015 Imagine Dragons participated in an installment of the „GRAMMY U. SoundChecks" series in Nashville, Tennessee. The band performed live and also engaged in a discussion and answer session with students.

After playing 15 Shows in 3 days at the South by Southwest Festival (SXSW) it shredded Dan´s voice. He had a polyp on one of his vocal cords that needed surgery.

The only time, that Imagine Dragons have ever been booed by their fans, was in Miami, where Dan mistakenly shouted: „ORLANDOOOO".... The crowd booed in response, but he made an immediate come back by pretending it was a joke, and soon won the crowd over by screaming „MIIAAAAMMII".

The very first time they played in Los Angeles, they had to pay the promoter $100 because not enough people came to see the band.

Dan did the Ice Bucket Challenge in Hamburg, Germany, where the weather was a cold and rainy 13 degree Celsius. He then went on to perform Radioactive in his soaking wet clothes.

In March 2021, as a celebration of the band being together for 10 years, Imagine Dragons provided a scholarship for refugees, immigrants or first generation Americans with the total value of $12.000. In cooperation with bold.org, the band announced the four winners (Israel, Trishna, Sai and Hiniye) in November 2021.

At one early point in their career, when Imagine Dragons chose to attend a celebrity afterparty, they noted to each other, 'we don't belong here' as they arrived on foot amongst limos and luxury cars.

Dan once joked in an interview that they thought about calling themselves 3D1B, because the band consists of three Dan´s and one Ben.

The band don´t really listen to their own music unless they're on a stage performing it. That helps keeps the music fresh for them, Dan revealed in an Interview.

While filming the On Top Of The World video, Dan Reynolds insisted on doing a stunt scene himself. He had to fall off a ladder onto limestone several times before the scene was perfect.

Dan said in an interview, that the currently unreleased song, Clouds was „the birth song of ID".

Whenever Dan picks up the microphone on the drum set and talks into it, you know something has gone wrong. Only crew members and the other band members can hear what he's saying.

The band take fish oil capsules to help improve their immune system whilst touring.

There are rumors about unreleased/maybe not even existing songs like Stars or Crash Course. It's a myth in the fandom. Update: At a concert in the early days of the band, they gave a CD called „Imagine Dragons Velour Sampler" to the fans. A demo version of Stars is featured on this album, so this song is no longer a myth.

In their early years, Imagine Dragons used to invite fans via Twitter, or sometimes during concerts, to play video games with them on their tour bus.

During the Evolve tour, Platz and Ben got similar tattoos. After they finished their show in Salt Lake City, Utah, en tour to Kansas, they stopped at the „Certified Tattoo Studio" in Colorado to get a tattoo of a fire breathing dragon, water skiing on a shark-filled ocean. Ben´s tattoo is on his thigh, whereas Platz´s sits on his flank.

In 2016, Imagine Dragons flew to Utah on their own dime and did a benefit concert along with other bands like the Neon Trees. Proceeds went to help Corey Fox, who needed a kidney transplant. Corey is the owner of Club Velour, where the band had one of their first public performances. The singer of the band, The Moths and the Flames, Brandon Robins, who had also one of their first public performances at the Velour, donated the organ to Corey. To find the performances on YouTube, search for #fixthefox.

X Ambassadors and Imagine Dragons share a special relationship... Imagine Dragons heard their song „Unconsolable" on local radio while touring in the Southeast. After learning that they were unsigned, they introduced them to Alex da Kid. Not only did ID help the young band to get a record deal, Dan Reynolds also co-wrote the song „Stranger" for their first EP and X Ambassadors were also an opening act at some shows for Imagine Dragons´ Into the Night Tour. A few years later, in June 2016, X Ambassadors and Imagine Dragons created the song „Sucker for Pain" along with other artists like Lil Wayne, Wiz Khalifa, Logic and Ty Dolla Sign, the band and X Ambassadors created this track for the Suicide Squad movie soundtrack.

Their very first videos, in 2009/2010, were shot by Matt Eastin on a Canon 5D D-SLR camera. He recorded the audio with a handheld boom mic. „I remember the band looking at the footage on the back of my D-SLR and they were really exited because they'd never had a video before" Eastin said in an interview.

The Uptight music video lost the band a record deal signing. Some label was interested, but after they saw the homemade music video for Uptight they were out. And now they will regret their decision deeply.

In their early days as a band, Imagine Dragons had to figure out their sound. Dan explained the method in an interview: "We rented an apartment together with the little bit of money we made from doing cover gigs, and we put a big whiteboard on the wall, and everybody wrote down five albums that were their all-time favorites". The band then listened to the albums to better understand each others musical preferences and to find a common path.

To make the music video for Roots realistic, the band provided Matt Eastin with real childhood photos and videos. Dan Reynolds even gave the director his hotel key card to so the crew could film him as soon as he woke up. The crew waited in Dan´s hotel room in the dark for about an hour to shoot this scene.

As a prank, in Switzerland, a band member threw their keyboard player from the Night Visions Tour, Ryan Walker (whose nickname is „Wolf") into a fountain.

An Egyptian start-up uses an Imagine Dragons song for it´s company name. Ahmad Hammouda and Seif Amr named their Cairo-based digital investment platform „Thndr" (pronounced Thunder). Ahmad explained the decision to use this name for their 2020 start-up with a lightning moment at the gym, "I listened to this song while he used the treadmill and he thought it´s a good name, because thunder, lightning implies speed."

Dan admitted in an interview, "We thought it would be funny to put on our rider* that we wanted a butler monkey, just to see if people were reading it.... They brought in a live monkey dressed up like a butler. So we all took pictures with it, except for Wayne, who is deathly afraid of monkeys. Now we´ve changed it to a penguin. We´ve had a few stuffed penguins."

* side note: a rider is a performance contract with which artists can request anything like special flowers, snacks,..

Let's do another game... so, what term does not fit in?

- ▶ I Bet My Life
- ▶ Second Chances
- ▶ Bleeding Out
- ▶ The Fall

- ▶ Dog
- ▶ Tattoo
- ▶ Atlanta Hawks
- ▶ Jazz

- ▶ Cutthroat
- ▶ Next To Me
- ▶ Roots
- ▶ On Top Of The World

- ▶ I Don´t Know Why
- ▶ Mouth Of The River
- ▶ Start Over
- ▶ Friction

- ▶ Sunnie Rae
- ▶ Wolfgang
- ▶ Valentine
- ▶ River

- ▶ Berklee
- ▶ Insomnia
- ▶ Ford Mustang
- ▶ Gold (color)

Milestones Of Imagine Dragons´ Career

2008

- Imagine Dragons released their first EP: „Speak to me".

2009

- The first gig as the new formed band Imagine Dragons: „I remember it very well. I remember we had all moved to Vegas, I think it was June 1 even, the day our first rehearsal was, and we had already planned a gig for June... 6, I want to say. We had set ourselves up for the pace we were gonna set ourselves very early on, it was pedal to the metal right from the beginning. We had to have material so we wrote together and practiced for 8 to 10 hours each of those days and got a few songs together so that we could play. Our first gig was interesting. It was at a rock club; it was called Sinister Rock Club. I think it's since closed down because someone got shot there, so it was not the best place probably in Las Vegas to play. But it was memorable." Wayne Sermon said in an Interview. He also mentioned, that during their first ever performance Ben turned on his amp and it started smoking and exploded on stage. „It was pretty awful," he added „We had to borrow someone else's amp to do our performance.

- Imagine Dragons took part in the Utah's got Talent Festival in June 2009. They won and became one of five local music acts to open for Kelly Clarkson at a concert at Utah Valley University's Brent Brown Ballpark, which took place on June 11, 2009.

- The band performed in Oct 2009 at the Bite of Las Vegas Music and Food Festival. They won the third place of the Battle of the Bite competition, which is a battle of bands showcase within the Bite of Las Vegas Festival. Later, when Train frontman Patrick Monahan had to pull out with a sore throat, just before they were due to be on stage, the organizers chose Imagine Dragons to fill the line up. This was the first time they performed in front of more than 20.000 people. „That moment had the greatest impact in our career" Ben said in an interview.

2010

- From the end of 2009, and right through the whole of 2010, Imagine Dragons completed their first ever tour by driving around various location in their bus, the self named „Dragon Wagon". Their Imagine Dragons Tour led them from LA, Provo, Las Vegas, San Francisco, American Fork, Santa Barbara, Salt Lake City to San Diego and Hermosa Beach.

- Additionally, they made their first TV appearance on FOX news and at the PBS program, Vegas in Tune.

- The band also performed at a few shows at SXSW 2010, including the BMI Official Showcase to increase their popularity. The South by Southwest Festival is a conglomeration of film, interactive media, music festival and conferences which takes place in Austin, Texas.

- Imagine Dragons became more famous by playing their most popular songs like Look How Far We've Come at musical festivals such as the New Noise Festival in Santa Barbara. They also performed at the Neon Reverb Festival, a nonprofit event without major sponsors, run by volunteers and helped out by local bands who play for free.

- Of course they were also again a part of the Bite of Las Vegas Festival and the Fork Fest, which is a music and art festival in Wayne´s hometown.

- Imagine Dragons were also noticed by the local press in 2010 and were named „Best Local Indie Band of 2010" by Las Vegas Weekly and „Las Vegas´ must-see Act" by Las Vegas City Life.

2011

- The 3rd EP „It´s Time" was released on March 12, 2011. The title track has been used by commercials and for series, documentaries and on TV events. The album was awarded „Best CD of 2011" by Vegas Seven Magazine.

- Imagine Dragons played their first international gig at the Bergenfest (April 2011). They had applied online to a competition and were chosen out of 2000 other bands to fly to Norway. An early version of "Hear Me" convinced the man in charge, Martin.

- Andrew and Brittany Tolman decided to leave the band and go back to college. Daniel Platzman was then recruited by Ben McKee as the new drummer. Andrew and Brittany played their last gig as members of Imagine Dragons on July, 29th in South Point, Ohio, USA.

- Theresa Flaminio, another Berklee graduate, joined the band in August 2011 as a keyboard player.

- In summer 2011, Imagine Dragons got the attention of Producer Alex da kid. Wayne spoke in an interview about their experiences working and bonding with him. „It was really simple, he just wrote us one day and said, "Hey, I like your music, why don't you come to LA and write with me for a day and see what happens?" And that's what we did. We went in there and it was just easy. Probably the number one way you can tell if something's going to work, if it's easy to write with somebody, if it's not a chore to write eight bars of music, if it just works naturally. It's kind of the way me and Dan were when we first met. It was easy to write together. And we felt that with Alex da Kid too. As a producer he's really great because he knows when to step back and he knows when to be really involved."

- The band had received record deals previously, but declined them because they wanted to stay independent. They accepted Alex da Kid's offer because he didn't want to change anything about the band, he just wanted to do things on a bigger scale.

- Dan called Wayne at 4 am to tell him, he thinks, Alex da Kid might really sign them. Wayne and Alex were at a hotel in Park City joining Wayne´s Dad (who had a conference in the city) when he got the call. Wayne said, this was one of this top 3 happiest moments in his life.

- In November 2011 Imagine Dragons announced the signing of a recording contract with Interscope Records and a plan to work with producer Alex da Kid on their first studio album.

2012

- In January 2012 Theresa Flaminio left the band.

- Imagine Dragons´ first music video It´s Time debuted on April 17, 2012. The video reached Number 1 on Yahoo Musics Top Video.

- The song It´s Time was performed by the band on such legendary shows like The Tonight Show with Jay Leno, on Jimmy Kimmel Live! and on Late Night with Jimmy Fallon (notable for being broadcast during Hurricane Sandy).

- The band finished their first studio album Night Visions at Studio X at the Palm Casino Resort and released it on September 4, 2012. The album peaked at Number 2 on the Billboard 200 Chart with first week sales of 83.000 copies.... The highest charting for a debut rock album since 2006.

- Imagine Dragons started their first big tour from September 5, until November 16, 2012. They supported the band Awolnation on their 40 date tour as their opening act. This stint was called The Fall Tour to promote their album Night Visions.

2013

- In February 2013, the 145-date worldwide Night Visions tour started.

- On March 4 Tyler Robinson, a 16 year old big fan of Imagine Dragons, passed away after a long fight due to „Rhabdomyosarcoma", a rare form of cancer. The band formed the „Tyler Robinson Foundation" to support families that face the burden of pediatric cancer.

- The band released their first DVD: Imagine Dragons: The Making of Night Visions on September 17, 2013, exclusively on iTunes. (The documentary debuted on VH1 Palladia at the end of 2012.)

- The band performed a medley of Demons and Radioactive at the American Music Awards (AMA´s) on November 24.

- Imagine Dragons provided several songs for film soundtracks. The song for Ready, Aim, Fire for Iron Man 3 in April 2013, the song Who We Are for The Hunger Games: Catching Fire Original soundtrack, in June 2013, and they released Monster for the Soundtrack to the game Infinity Blade III.

2014

- On January 25, the band performed the song „Revolution" at The Beatles Tribute Grammy Ceremony in front of Yoko Ono, Sir Paul McCartney and Ringo Starr.

- At The Grammy Awards Imagine Dragons performed their song Radioactive in an explosive mash-up with Kendrick Lamar´s „M.A.A.D. City" on January 26.

- At the 56th Grammy Ceremony, Imagine Dragons had nominations in two categories, Record of the Year and Best Rock Performance. They won the award for Best Rock Performance.

- The band were asked to do the music score for the film Transformers: Age of Extinction. It's a bitterly cold Thursday in Boston, even for March — the day's highest temperature is well below freezing. Platzman and his bandmates are squeezed into a taxicab somewhere near Berklee, heading along Newbury Street toward the venue for that night's show. Suddenly, a message from Mac Reynolds, the band's manager, pops up on someone's device: „Hey guys. Michael Bay wants to Skype with you in ten minutes. Is that cool?"

He wanted to collaborate with the band on the music of the 4th Transformers movie. Excited, the band started writing right in the cab. What if the guitar did this? What if the drums sounded like that? When they arrived at the venue, they began cobbling sounds together on a computer in the green room.

After sound check, they couldn't rush back fast enough to keep writing and recording. "We have a one-track mind. We're really bad at setting it down. And it's intense — if you step away, you'll miss out." The band was massively excited to work with Stephen Jablonsky and Hans Zimmer on the soundtrack for Transformers - Age of Extinction.

- They performed Battle Cry live at the world premiere of Transformers - Age of Extinction in Hong Kong with a great show (many drummers and fireworks) on June 19, 2014.

- The band performed just seven days later at the legendary Glastonbury festival in Pilton, England. All band members had great fun jumping in the famous mud pools, getting absolutely covered. The line up that year featured Metallica, The 1975, Lily Allen, Jake Bugg and Dolly Parton, amongst others.

- Imagine Dragons wrote and created the song Warriors along with Riot Games for League of Legends. It was the official theme song for the online battle arena video game. In October, the band performed live in Seoul for the League of Legends World Championship.

- Weird al Yankovic made a parody of Imagine Dragons´ Radioactive. In an Interview, Platz said: "Were all big Al fans. Ben´s first three live concerts are Weird Al and I used to perform his polkas at summer camp with my brother every summer. Polka your Eyes out is the Platzman family favorite"

- On November 22, 2014, the first TRF Gala was organized to help families with pediatric cancer. One of the highlights of the show was a live unplugged performance by Imagine Dragons. More than $300.000 were raised by this event.

2015

- Imagine Dragons did an advert for Target by performing their song Shots live during the 4 minute commercial break for the Grammy Awards on February 8, 2015.

- Their self-produced album Smoke + Mirrors was launched on February 17. The album was recorded at the bands own studio in Las Vegas. It was created together with Alexander Grant, better known as Alex da Kid. The band invested a tremendous amount of time and effort into its promotion and the following world tour.

- Imagine Dragons were the first musical guests to appear on the show The Muppets. They appeared on the episode „Pig Girls Don't Cry", which aired September 22, 2015, and performed the song Roots.

- On November 10, Imagine Dragons frontman Dan Reynolds opened up to fans during a concert at Leeds Arena, UK about his Ankylosing Spondylitis disease.

2016

- Imagine Dragons created their first ever instrumental track, Wings. It is only accessible through the in-game soundtrack to NBA 2K17. This soundtrack also features the songs Friction and the Jorgen Odegard remix of Gold. Wings was released on September 20, 2016

- Dan participated in an all star song to protest the unauthorized use of music in presidential campaigns. He joined Josh Groban, Michael Bolton, Cindy Lauper, Usher, Sheryl Crow and many more on the song: „Don´t Use Our Song". The mix of parody and protest song was published in July 2016.

2017

- The band performed at Vegas Strong, a charity concert to pay tribute to the victims of the shooting that happened on October 1 in Las Vegas. The concert featured Boyz II Men, Cirque du Soleil, David Copperfield and the Killers to name just a few artists.

- Imagine Dragons streamed a concert of their Evolve tour live via Twitter. The performance took place in Montreal, Canada and was streamed in cooperation with Live Nation.

2018

- A collaboration between Imagine Dragons and Kygo was announced on June 12, 2018. The song Born To Be Yours was released 3 days later.

- At the release of their album Origins on November 7, the band incorporated a little award show. A few very special and important people in the bands´ lives received Origins awards. Each band member told stories about the prize winners, explaining how they had affected their lives. Of course the band also performed tracks form their new album, along with some classics. This event was titled Origins Experience, and was streamed live on YouTube.

- Imagine Dragon teamed up with Angry Birds to raise awareness of their non-profit charity TRF. In the game, that they created, you have to help baby birds, known as hatchlings, set up their rock concert by completing different challenges.

2019

- Oculus announced they were teaming up with Imagine Dragons to create a 10 track Imagine Dragons Music Pack for the popular virtual reality game „Beat Saber". In the game, you are a virtual Samurai, using a couple of light swords to slice blocks that are coming at you to the beat of music. The music pack includes songs from all four studio albums.

- On the 1 of June in Madrid, Spain, the UEFA Champions League Final opening ceremony featured a spectacular live performance by Imagine Dragons.

- Las Vegas Mayor, Carolyn Goodman, attended the TRF Rise Up Gala at the Wynn and proclaimed September 6 as National Imagine Dragons Day in Las Vegas for „these generous souls and everything they do for humanity".

2020

- The album Evolve was announced as „the most streamed album of All Time" by a group on the streaming platform Spotify. (September 2020)

- For the first time since it started in 2014, the TRF Rise up Gala had to be postponed until 2021 due to the worldwide pandemic.

- Radioactive is announced as the 3rd best selling song of ALL TIME in pure copies in the US. The song has sold over 8.8 million units in pure sales and is certified as Diamond in the Country. (November 2020)

- Imagine Dragons have more than 30 millions followers on Spotify. Making them the most followed group of all time on the music platform. (November 2020)

- Imagine Dragons sold the rights to their songs for more than $ 100 million. Concord Music Publishing has and Universal Music Publishing Group now share the rights to the band's songs.

- Billboard announced „Believer" as Goggle's 5th most searched song by humming.

- Imagine Dragons hid a secret link to a page on their website. After entering a password, you were taken to another page (Deep Cuts) containing old, partly unreleased songs, plus a 1 hour backstage documentary of the bands Smoke + Mirrors album.

2021

- In March, Imagine Dragons sent four different cryptic videos out to their fans, all over the world. When the videos had been deciphered, the release date for the two new singles, Follow You and Cutthroat, of the long awaited new album was revealed.

- Recording Mercury Act 1 was different from anything, Imagine Dragons had ever done. The band quarantined for a month, and the whole production team got tested every second day for COVID-19.

- Imagine Dragons announced in April, a cover competition for their singles „Follow You" and „Cutthroat". Every adult (18+) or group could take part and upload a video with his/her/their contribution. After a first round of public voting, the band finally decides who wins the price which was a zoom video call from the band and $20.000.

- During the promotion for Mercury Act 1, the band discovered a new platform: TikTok. They regularly posted short videos and also collaborations with other famous TikTokers.

- In August 2021, the band streamed their first ever live charity event on their YouTube channel. Using the hashtag #FreeTheFox, Imagine Dragons raised money for Corey Fox. He has owned the legendary Velour in Utah since January 2006. Many bands started their career there and ID had their first performances on stage at this venue. Due to the lockdown in the COVID crisis, Corey´s club had to deal with some serious financial struggles. At the charity live stream, Imagine Dragons performed a few acoustic songs, took phone calls from fans and answered questions. Neon Trees also performed a song and Corey Fox told stories about incidents from the beginning of Imagine Dragons. For the 16th anniversary of the Velour Live Music Gallery, Dan Reynolds performed a few songs at the club and surprised Corey Fox with a „paid in full" mortgage note in Mai 2022.

- Almost 3 years after their last performance, Imagine Dragons performed at the Kulture Ball in Birmingham which is a charity event benefiting Platz´ and Ben´s non-profit organization, KultureCity..

- In November 2021, Imagine Dragons became the first band in history with 60 entries in Billboard's Hot Rock & Alternative songs chart. The band achieved this milestone with the song Enemy, for the Netflix animated series, Arcane.

2022

- In February, Imagine Dragons started their biggest world tour to date in Florida. This tour was the first time they linked a part of their show to an existing video. Actors, Rob Mc Ellenhey and his wife Kaitlin Olson joined the band on stage during their sold-out show in Los Angeles. Together they performed the story of the music video "Follow You" live.

- The band invited 600 fans to a cinema for an exclusive, private first look at their Sharks music video in Vienna. The event in July also included a listening to the new album Mercury Act 2 (one week prior to it´s release) and a question and answer session with the band.

- In 2022, the band became the first group ever with 4 songs certified with Diamond status. That is the highest certification of the „Recording Industry Association of America" (RIAA) and it is equal to the level of 10 million equivalent units by combining sales and streaming numbers (equates going Platinum 10 times). Radioactive reached this status in November 2020, Believer in May 2021, Demons in August 2021 and Thunder in July 2022.

Personalized confetti fell on the audience during the performance of "The Fall" on the Mercury tour.

We bet you're wondering, who threw Ryan Walker in the fountain in Switzerland?
Let's find out by solving this riddle:

1								
2								
3								
4								
5								

1) One of Ben McKee´s charities (abbreviation).
2) This artist created the album cover artwork for Smoke + Mirrors.
3) Imagine Dragons honored this boy by establishing a charity foundation.
4) This song is the product of Imagine Dragons´ second collaboration with RIOT Games.
5) This is where the music video for Imagine Dragons´ "Whatever It Takes" was filmed.

Imagine Dragons and video games

The band has a special connection to video games. Dan and Wayne in particular are crazy about this pastime. Both have played video games since childhood. Dan even refers to his Nintendo 64 as „God´s greatest gift to humanity" and Wayne loved his Commodore 64 console. Ben likes to stick to classic arcade games (Donkey Kong is his favorite) and Platz prefers online games like League Of Legends.

In the band's early days, they played video games in their Dragon Wagon before their performances, along with their fans. Around 2013, Dan found out about MOBA (Multiplayer Online Battle Arena) and used it to take his mind off his busy tour and press schedule. He admits that he „was terrible at it and the learning curve was super hard", but these were exactly the kind of games he enjoys to „decompress". He told Wayne about this type of game and soon, League Of Legends became a new obsession for them.

One day, one of Dan´s brother met someone who happened to work at League Of Legends studio Riot Games. The conversation soon went from „My brother plays this game too" to „Isn't your brother the singer for Imagine Dragons?". The studio contacted the band , who then visited the headquarters and met with the creators and other people involved in the development of League of Legends.

In 2014, Imagine Dragons created the song „Warriors" for League Of Legends and performed the song live at the LOL World Championship in Seoul. Dan mentioned in an interview, that the collaboration with Riot came organically and nothing was forced.

Imagine Dragons had just wrapped up their Night Visions World Tour when their manager, Mac Reynolds, told them, "Guys, we have this opportunity but it´s gonna go quick — just say yes or no". He spoke about a live performance with legendary Nintendo composer Koji Kindo. The very next day they were on stage with him at the first inaugural Game Awards 2014 in Las Vegas.

The band launched a Twitch channel in 2015. They were streaming their League Of Legends matches, interviews, and impromptu live performances via the Telestream Wirecast service. Mac Reynolds explains, "The band is always looking for ways to connect to fans on a personal level....

By live streaming from their Smoke + Mirrors Tour, they're able to take fans with them behind the scenes in locations around the world." The Project Manager of the band, Turner Pope came up with the idea of creating their own channel, which had more than 20,000 followers. Unfortunately, there is no way to watch the videos again

Mr. Linke, the creator and producer of the Netflix series Arcane, got in touch in 2019. He shared the premise and early randings with the band. The storyline of two sisters choosing a different life path and their internal and external conflict suited Imagine Dragons very well.

„I've never written a song about League Of Legends or Arcane.
I´m given these themes, I understand it and then I find my truth in it and write lyrically for myself - I can't write for someone else, I was never able to do that." explains Dan Reynolds in an Interview with nme.com.

Dan used the band's hiatus after the release of their fourth studio album, Origins, to learn C# programming. He took a few online courses and soon started making a bunch of mini-games. Though Dan said they were „terrible", his test player, Wayne, said that Dan was just being self-deprecating.

Making a game was something Dan dreamed of since he was a kid. So when he had an idea for a game, he didn't hesitate and put together a small team of about a dozen people. The team has been working on this for about 2 years and Dan can already say, that this was not his first and last game. "The process of making a game, to play it with just my friends and test it, that has been priceless." And now, we are patiently waiting for Dan to announce the release date.

Incidents During Live Performances

Dan has tore his pants on stage a few times. Once during his performance at the Lollapalooza Festival in Paris 2017 and a second time at the Vegas Strong Charity Concert in Las Vegas 2017. That wasn't a good year for his pants!

A fan ran onto stage during the performance of Radioactive at the Arena di Verona 2017. Security were fast and managed to catch him, however he did manage to damaged a drum, which meant the band had to play an alternative song (Song 2).

Dan fell down on the stage during a concert in 2015. Don't worry, he didn't hurt himself, he slipped, jumped back on his feet and continued to sing like nothing happened. „The Show must go on...“ must be his motto.

Ben and Platz pranked their opening band, Sunset Sons several times during the Smoke + Mirrors Tour by running onto the stage during their performance wearing disgusting masks!

In April 2013, during a performance of Radioactive in Berlin, Dan seriously hurt his hand by hitting the big drum too hard and he managed to break two fingers. He only realized when he noticed that his fingers were just hanging down but felt no pain right after the incident.

Due to his broken hand, Dan could not perform Radioactive as he usually would do. Instead, for a couple of shows (one of which was at Raleigh, North Carolina 05/08/2013) he was lifted up in the air by a cable and floated above the stage. He made a few artistic moves and smashed a drum which was hanging high up in the air!

The band wanted to perform Gold at the Mohegan Sun Area in November 2017. The music started, Dan walked toward the mic stand, to find the microphone was missing, by which time it was too late. He joked: „At least you know now, I sing everything“.

At the Colors of Ostrava Festival in 2017, Dan left a fan alone on stage and told him to dance whilst Dan was crowdsurfing and singing „Song 2".

At Lollapalooza in 2014, Dan Reynolds enthusiastically decided to crowd-surf the Argentinian audience. Not his best idea. The fans were so hyped from his energetic "Radioactive" performance that they nearly ripped his shirt and only the security saved Dan from being undressed by the crowd. After he got back on stage, he said, „I think I´m pregnant from crowd-surfing now".

After introducing the band, Dan wanted Wayne to do a Whistle-Guitar-Off at a concert in Miami Beach 2015. He whistled a melody and Wayne would play the exact same notes, on his guitar. Well, Wayne tried, but his guitar was off at the first try. A few minutes later, he mastered this little competition perfectly.

During their last performance of the Smoke + Mirrors Tour in Amsterdam at the Ziggo Dome Arena (February 2015), Imagine Dragons were joined on stage during the song, On Top Of The World, by a male cheerleader wearing a crop top, short skirt, and shaking pink pompoms. This was Rory Williams, lead singer of Imagine Dragons opening band Sunset Sons. He took revenge for Ben and Platz´s constant pranks during his band's performance. It´s fair to say that a lot of fun was had by all!

During their performance of the song Thunder, at the July 2017 St. Petersburg concert, the band were bombed by hundreds of paper airplanes, which were thrown on stage by fans.

Wayne Sermon changed his guitar solo for the Hopeless Opus/ Polaroid mashup and played Happy Birthday for Dan Reynolds at the concert in Mönchengladbach, Germany on July 14, 2022.

AWARDS

2013

American Music Awards

Nominated: New Artist of the year
Nominated: Favorite Band/Duo/Group - Pop/Rock
WON: Favorite Artist - Alternative Rock

MTV Europe Music Awards

Nominated: Best Push
Nominated: Best New

Teen Choice Awards

Nominated: Best Rock Group
Nominated: Best Rock Song (Radioactive)
Nominated: Best Music Breakout Group
Nominated: Summer Music Star: Group

2014

American Music Awards

Nominated: Artist of the Year
Nominated: Favorite Band/Duo/Group - Pop/Rock
WON: Favorite Artist - Alternative Rock

2014

Billboard Music Awards

Nominated: Top Artist
Nominated: Top Rock Song (Radioactive)
Nominated: Top Rock Song (Demons)
Nominated: Top Digital Song Artist
Nominated: Top Radio Song Artist
Nominated: Top Streaming Artist
Nominated: Top Digital Song (Radioactive)
Nominated: Top Hot 100 Song (Radioactive)
WON: Top Streaming Song (Audio) (Radioactive)
WON: Top Rock Album (Night Visions)
WON: Top Rock Artist
WON: Top Duo/Group
WON: Top Hot 100 Artist

Grammy Awards

Nominated: Record of the Year (Radioactive)
WON: Best Rock Performance (Radioactive)

iHeartRadio Music Awards

Nominated: Artist of the year
Nominated: Song of the Year (Radioactive)
Nominated: Best New Artist
WON: Alternative Rock Song of the Year (Demons)

MTV Europe Music Awards

Nominated: Best World Stage (Live Amsterdam)

Clio Awards - Music Partnership/Collaborations

WON: Use of Music - Licensed
BRONZE: „The Battle Back Home" - Demons

2014

People´s Choice Awards USA

Nominated: Favorite Song (Radioactive)
Nominated: Favorite Alternative Band
Nominated: Favorite Band
Nominated: Favorite Breakout Artist

Teen Choice Awards

Nominated: Rock Song (On Top Of The World)
WON: Rock Group

2015

People´s Choice Awards USA

Nominated: Favorite Group

Teen Choice Awards

Nominated: Music Group Male
Nominated: Rock Song (I Bet My Life)

2016

People´s Choice Awards

Nominated: Favorite Album (Smoke + Mirrors)
Nominated: Favorite Group

2017

American Music Awards

Nominated: Favorite Artist - Alternative Rock
WON: Favorite Band/Duo or Group - Pop/Rock

Billboard Music Awards

Nominated: Top Rock Song (Sucker For Pain)

MTV Europe Music Awards

Nominated: Best Alternative

Teen Choice Awards

Nominated: Rock Artist
Nominated: Song: Group (Believer)
Nominated: Summer Group
WON: Rock/Alternative Song (Believer)

2018

American Music Awards

Nominated: Artist of the year
Nominated: Favorite Band/Duo/Group - Pop/Rock
Nominated: Favorite Artist - Alternative Rock

2018

Billboard Music Awards

> Nominated: Top Hot 100 Artist
> Nominated: Top Song Sales Artist
> Nominated: Top Radio Songs Artist
> Nominated: Top Rock Song (Thunder)
> Nominated: Top Radio Song (Believer)
> Nominated: Top Selling Song (Thunder)
> Nominated: Top Selling Song (Believer)
> **WON: Top Rock Album (Evolve)**
> **WON: Top Duo/Group**
> **WON: Top Rock Song (Believer)**
> **WON: Top Rock Artist**

Grammy Awards

> Nominated: Best Pop Vocal Album (Evolve)
> Nominated: Best Pop Duo/Group Performance
> (Thunder)

iHeartRadio Music Awards

> Nominated: Best Duo/Group of the Year
> Nominated: Alternative Rock Song of the Year
> (Believer)
> Nominated: Alternative Rock Song of the Year
> (Thunder)
> **WON: Alternative Rock Artist of the Year**

MTV Europe Music Awards

> Nominated: Best US Act
> Nominated: Best Rock

2018

People´s Choice Awards

    Nominated: Concert Tour of 2018
    Nominated: Group of 2018

Teen Choice Awards

    Nominated: Song Group
    Nominated: Summer Group
    WON: Rock Artist
    WON: Rock/Alternative Song (Whatever It Takes)

2019

American Music Awards

    Nominated: Favorite Artist - Alternative Rock

Billboard Music Awards

    Nominated: Top Rock Song (Whatever It Takes)
    Nominated: Top Rock Song (Natural)
    Nominated: Top Rock Album (Origins)
    Nominated: Top Song Sales Artist
    Nominated: Top Duo/Group
    WON: Top Rock Artist

iHeartRadio Music Awards

    Nominated: Best Duo/Group of the Year
    Nominated: Alternative Rock Song of the Year
        (Natural)
    WON: Alternative Rock Artist of the Year
    WON: Most Thumbed-up Artist of the Year

2019

MTV Europe Music Awards

Nominated: Best Rock

People´s Choice Awards

Nominated: Group of 2019

Teen Choice Awards

Nominated: Rock Artist
Nominated: Song Group (Bad Liar)
Nominated: Rock Song (Natural)

2020

Billboard Music Awards

Nominated: Top Rock Artist
Nominated: Top Rock Song (Bad Liar)

iHeartRadio Music Awards

Nominated: Best Duo/Group of the Year
Nominated: Alternative Rock Artist of the Year

2021

MTV Video Music Awards

    Nominated: Best Alternative Video (Follow You)

NRJ Music Awards

    Nominated: International Duo/Group of the Year
    Nominated: International Song of the Year
          (Follow You)
    WON: Award of Honor

2022

Billboard Music Awards

    Nominated: Top Duo/Group
    Nominated: Top Rock Artist
    Nominated: Top Rock Album (Mercury Act 1)
    Nominated: Top Rock Song (Follow You)

Clio Awards - Music Partnership/Collaborations

    WON: Music Marketing
    Silver: „Arcane League of Legends"
    Enemy (with JID)

For the sake of clarity, only the most popular awards have been mentioned here.

So, let's have some fun here...

Can you guess the song by emoji´s?

1) 🚬 + 🥚 _____

2) 👻 _____

3) 👂🏄 _____

4) ∞🌙 _____

5) 🕺⬛ _____

6) 🍂🍃 _____

7) 👄👊 _____

8) ☝️🌍 _____

9) 💧💧💧 _____

10) ☀️♏😎 _____

11) 🖤 _____

12) 🍩➡️🗣️ _____

13) 111111000110110 _____

14) 🐬 _____

15) ➡️🏝️ _____

16) 🌅⬆️ _____

17) 🔥❌ _____

18) 🐬🐬 _____

19) ☠️🦴 _____

20) ⏭️🏄 _____

Maybe I´m breaking up with myself
Maybe I´m thinking I should just keep to
The things that I've been told
Wait for the colors to turn to gold
Do you know?
Do you know?
You're all I know

The Fall
Smoke + Mirrors

Charity By Imagine Dragons

<u>TRF (Tyler Robinson Foundation)</u>

We assume you bought this book because you wanted to know more about Imagine Dragons. If you really want to know everything about the band, you should also know about their connection to the Tyler Robinson Foundation. This non-profit was founded by Imagine Dragons and the Robinson family to honor a young man, a passionate fan of the band, who battled cancer and very sadly lost.

Let's have a look back to fall 2012. Imagine Dragons was releasing their debut album Night Visions and a few miles away, in Salt Lake City, the 17 year old Tyler had just received fantastic news: He was declared cancer-free! Yayyyy!!! It had been a hard, stony road he had to go through. "The path to heaven runs through miles of clouded hell." Oh, Tyler could really relate to these words.

Growing up with 5 siblings, Tyler was the youngest and was the most spoiled. Although he received more things, more attention, he wasn't the type of kid who annoyed others. He never bragged about things and never complained. He also had this special gift, the ability to connect to adults as well as to people his age. Tyler loved the film "Bugs Life" so when his family visited Disneyland one day, they put him on the Bugs-Life-Ride. But this poor little guy, only 5/6 years of age, was so afraid that they had to take him off.

Tyler and his family were really close, but he shared a very special bond with his brother, Jesse, who was six years older. That bond was music. When Jesse was in high school, he introduced Tyler to 80´s rock as well as classic stuff, and in return Tyler shared with his brother music of his age group.

Tyler (Ty) and his older brother Jesse

This was the time, when Tyler got sick. At age 11, he scraped his knee and got a Staphylococcal infection. It was a very serious disease because the infection spread through his whole body and starts to attack and to shut down his organs. Tyler was in intensive care for 6 weeks, during which he needed to undergo eleven surgeries and he actually came closer to dying during this infection than he did during his cancer treatments. There were a couple of moments when the family were told by the doctors to come to the hospital to say goodbye because they were thinking Tyler wouldn't make it through the night. That never happened during the cancer treatment.

But Tyler was a fighter, he never gave up and he got healthy again. Life went back to normal, Tyler went to school, had fun with his many friends and he had also good chances with the ladies. But he also appreciated the love and care of his family. Then, one day, Tyler was suffering from back pain. He wasn't worried about it because he had been back-lifting. "I've done it a hundred times, don´t worry, it will be fine" he told his older brother. His mom started panicking that the staph infection might have come back so, when the pain wasn't better the next day, Tyler and his mom went to see a doctor.

They went to the hospital, where Tyler had spent months with his staph infection. After some tests, Tyler and his mother received the devastating diagnosis: He had cancer. It was a muscular cancer, "Rhabdomyosarcoma," that had metastasized all over his body. 95% of his bone marrow was infected with cancer cells. He had so many tumors on his spine, little, tiny tumors, that the doctor couldn't even count them on the X-rays. When Tyler and his mom drove home that day, both were in a state of shock. It was the only time, Tyler had cried.

The entire family was desperate, shocked, frustrated and angry. Ty just got his life back, and now, everything starts again. It just wasn't fair. Tyler and his brother, Jesse, had a little ritual, which they did several times during his staph infection. Jesse walked into Ty's room with a mixture of rootbeer and milk, shouting "Yo, bro's in the house". This became their thing, almost like they had their own little club. But this time, Jesse tried to connect to his brother with music. When Imagine Dragons´ song "It´s Time" played on his iPod, it really triggered Tyler. Although Jesse had tried to comfort his younger brother already, the band had definitely found the better words: "The path to heaven runs through miles of clouded hell." These lines made Tyler turn 180 degrees. From sad, complaining, angry, upset to being positive regardless of the sad situation. Whenever things were tough, they just had to remind themselves, "That's the path. This is just a perspective check."

Things were tough. Through chemotherapy, radiation, Ty lost his hair and felt sick. At this phase of Tyler´s illness, Jesse and his best friend, Zack, found out that Imagine Dragons were going to perform at the Club Velour in Provo, Utah. The friends immediately had the same thought: Tyler´s gotta go. After Jesse tried to reach out to the band through their management, Zack got in contact with them using Facebook. And this idea worked.

On the evening of the concert, Zack and Jesse snuck out of the hospital with Tyler to take him to the venue, to a room with 300 sweaty college kids. That's the worst place for a kid with cancer. Jesse knew it wasn't a good idea, but his heart told him the opposite. He had informed Tyler about the plan to attend an Imagine Dragons concert beforehand. Tyler was excited and agreed to the plan. Jesse remembers, "I didn't know how long he's gonna live so I felt like this is his only opportunity to meet his favorite band or at least see them play then."

They had such an amazing experience at the venue. Not only did frontman, Dan Reynolds dedicate "It´s Time" to Tyler, he also sang the song with him! Tyler was lifted on his brother's shoulders and he rocked Club Velour. Ty had the time of his life, he was literally radiating energy and zest for living that night.

Tyler and Dan exchanged phone numbers backstage after the show and the band put them on their list. So anytime they came to a show, they just got in. Whenever the band was in town, Tyler and his family hung out with them and their families. Tyler and Dan talked the most. The band had a guest appearance at the Jay Leno Show. While they were backstage, they were on the phone with Tyler. "Oh, we have to go out on stage and meet Jay Leno, we gotta go, they were calling us". They hung up, running out and then Tyler could watch them on TV. And he was just like beaming....

Dan and Wayne met Tyler after the show

Tyler went through many cancer treatments and they actually went picture perfect. From the beginning to end everything went perfectly. His cancer treatment went so well that he was an international case and was studied by other doctors. His body reacted so well to the treatments, that he was declared cancer free in fall 2012.

Again, just like after his staph infection, Tyler began to re-build his life. He went back to school and started to make future plans. Four months after he had left the hospital, he collapsed in the bathroom and fell into a coma. At the hospital they found several tumors in his brain that were inoperable. Tyler never woke up again.

Tyler Robinson passed away on March 4, 2013. His family informed the band about this tragedy and on that same day, at night, Dan called Tyler´s brother, Jesse. They shared their sympathy and how sorry they were. Then they said, "We wanna start a foundation and we want to do it with you guys. We will call it Tyler Robinson Foundation. We don´t know, what exactly we´re gonna do but let's do something. We´ve been given this worldwide platform with music and we want do good by it."

Jesse Robinson with Imagine Dragons

They wanted it to be different, not just like every other non-profit. So they developed a unique program to help families with pediatric cancer by not only providing financial aid to the families (upwards to $50,000 for every family who stay with the organization for 1-3 years on average) but they also get training from financial experts on how to budget and to manage their finances in the future to stand on their own two feet. The band was just about to skyrocket, so their manager (and Dan´s brother) Mac Reynolds took care of the just founded organization. So it´s a fact that TRF wouldn't exist without Mac.

Things went really crazy when the band dedicated their music video "Demons" in May 2013 to Tyler. Imagine Dragons used the footage from Tyler´s and Dan´s concert experience in Provo for the last few seconds of Demons. The doors at TRF were opening left, right, left, right with so many collaboration requests from companies, cool festivals and really unique opportunities that non-profit organizations normally don't get.

Since then, many great things have happened. There´s the annual TRF Gala, various events, collaboration with artists and companies, merchandise, and competitions. We will tell you more about some of these amazing things in the next chapter of the book. TRF follows the motto of their gala: "Rise up". With the help of their board, international volunteers and donators, the Tyler Robinson Foundation is continually growing. They've expanded to Canada, Mexico, Europe and also South Africa. But before they step foot into a new region, the organization makes sure that there are partner hospitals to help them find families, an infrastructure with volunteers and enough donors. This is important because the money raised in a country stays in that country. So every dollar, that is raised for example in Canada stays in Canada for Canadian families.

We will leave the last words of this article to Jesse Robinson, Tyler´s older brother, who was so kind to answer all our questions patiently. "I think, I will speak in the name of Tyler when I say this: TRF is less about Tyler, it´s more about everyone else. This is not a foundation to celebrate one person, this is a foundation to help families that are struggling."

Imagine Dragons´ tweet

TRF hosts an annual gala that includes an auction, a stylish dinner, and a live acoustic performance by Imagine Dragons. All proceeds of the gala went to the foundation.

The band also tries to raise awareness and money for TRF in different ways, for example:

- Together with Hard Rock Cafe, Imagine Dragons created a signature series merchandise program. The band designed T-shirts and Pins for sale in 2015.

- On February 5, 2016, the band launched a smartphone game called Stage Rush.

- In conjunction with Zappo, in 2018, the band created a Limited-Edition COTU Classic Superga sneaker. The design was made by Tim Cantor, the creator of the Smoke + Mirrors album cover.

- Also in 2018, Imagine Dragons teamed up with the creators of Angry Birds to develop a game together.

- The band were busy in 2018... they also teamed up with Crowdrise for an amazing competition: „Win a chance for you and three friends to attend a Meet and Greet with Imagine Dragons on New Year's Eve". This also included flights for four people, two nights stay at The Cosmopolitan and a $350 gift card to BOA/Sushi Roku.

- In 2019, there was the first-ever Battle for Vegas Charity softball event.

- Also a Charity „Series of Poker" event happened in 2019 in Las Vegas (with Ben McKee)

- And in 2020, a chance to meet and greet Imagine Dragons and join them on a zero-gravity flight. Additionally, there's a chance to win a new X-Box in a special design.

- In 2022, you could donate to TRF to increase your chances to win a trip to Spain to see ID, including a roundtrip airfare & 4 * night hotel stay for 2 people, pre-show dinner at one of the bands favorite local restaurants, 2 VIP passes to an ID show and seats in the friends & family section. A signed guitar and signed poster of the band were also part of the raffle.

These are only a few examples of the bands commitment to TRF.

Now don´t you understand
That I´m never changing who I am
So this is where you fell
And I am left to sell
The path to heaven runs through miles of clouded hell
Right to the top
Don´t look back

It´s Time
Night Visions

Kim Gradisher

Tyler Robinson Foundation

As you know, all proceeds from sales of this book go to TRF. We´ve already told you about Tyler Robinson and his bond with Imagine Dragons, but there is so much more that needs to be mentioned about this amazing organization. Kim Gradisher, Executive Director of TRF, was so kind to answer a few questions.

The Tyler Robinson Foundation helps families with pediatric cancer by providing financial aid. How exactly does this work?

Social workers at our 50+ partner hospitals submit grant applications that are carefully reviewed by our Family Selection Committee and TRF staff. Families are selected and welcomed into the program with the appropriate grants to best assist them and are provided the option of meeting with a financial advisor. Grant funds are then used to pay directly for families' appropriate non-medical expenses for one year based on the grant they received. These expenses can include travel, food, auto, insurance, rent, and mortgage expenses to name a few.

TRF organizes the famous TRF Gala every year. Could you tell us a bit about this event?

It is our biggest fundraiser every year and allows us to provide grants to our many families. TRF supporters, families, and fans are welcomed to enjoy a night of fun and music, featuring a performance by TRF founders, Imagine Dragons. We look forward to this event every year as it is the culmination of all of the TRF board and staff's hard work and a celebration of our TRF families.

Are there any other ways to support TRF apart from donations?

We have our Pen Pal Program, which you can learn more about at trf.org/penpal. We accept notes of encouragement, art, and more that we then pass along to our TRF kids throughout the year. The kids love receiving them and seeing that there are people out there rooting for them in their cancer journey.

TRF already teamed up with a lot of awesome people and companies like Tim Cantor, Hard Rock Cafe, the creators of Angry Birds, Beat Saber and many others. Is there any person or company you would love to cooperate with in the future?

We are always honored and humbled by the opportunities that have arisen for us to work with so many amazing people and companies looking to make a difference in the lives of pediatric cancer families.

There isn't any one person or company we particularly want to work with in the future, but we have had so many interesting and fun opportunities pop up and are always open to the new possibilities that they bring to the table to help our families.

85 cents of every dollar donated goes directly to the affected families. This is incredible! You can be really proud of your team! And the families need as much support as possible as they are facing the burden of pediatric cancer. Is there any story you want to share with us? Something heartwarming, cute or funny that happened with one of these families?

We have been able to interact with so many families over the years, both virtually and in real life. One of the most memorable moments for our team was an acoustic sing-along with Imagine Dragons and some of our TRF families in 2019. Being able to meet and interact with so many of our families in one place, with such a fun purpose was a memorable moment that we all cherish.

Thank you for your time!

It´s great to read about TRF, but we recommend a visit to www.trf.org to get more information about the Pen Pal Program, to have a look at previous TRF Galas or to get some nice, unique merchendise from the TRF store.

But the band supports other causes too......

They were part of a fundraising event (Meet and Greet) with „Do the Write Thing: National Campaign to Stop Violence" to raise money to reduce violence and its impact for the lives of young people.

On February 5, 2014, the band performed at the „Amnesty´s Bringing Human Rights Home Concert" at Barclays Center in Brooklyn to support Amnesty International.

In November 2014, Imagine Dragons performed a surprise show with three acoustic songs in front of the Bellagio Hotel in Las Vegas to support the „Playing It Forward" program. This is a street performance music series where $100.000 is donated to the artists charity of choice. The band performed It's Time, I Bet My Life and Radioactive for the benefit of music programs in local schools.

Imagine Dragons have teamed up with SAP and Apple to create the „One4 Project". Apple, Imagine Dragons and the bands label KIDinaKORNER/Interscope donated their respective proceeds from paid downloads of the song I Was Me to the UN Refugee Agency. SAP will donate 10 cents for every download up to the first 5 million downloads from iTunes. „The song I Was Me is about people trying to regain their life, which is exactly what millions of people are going through right now" Dan Reynolds said in a short video clip explaining the bands involvement in the cause. This happened in October 2015.

On December 18, 2015, Imagine Dragons were one of many artists who released a special cover of the song I Love You All The Time by Eagles of Death Metal, in response to the November 13, 2015, attacks in Paris. All the proceeds from the song were donated to „Friends of Foundation de France".

Along with other musicians, like Mary J. Blidge, Jason Derulo, Selena Gomez, Halsey, Jennifer Lopez, Britney Spears to name just a few, the band sang the song „Hands" - A Song For Orlando. The proceeds of the sales in the United States benefited Equality Florida Pulse Victims Fund, the GLBT Community Center of Central Florida and GLAAD. Hands is a musical tribute to the 49 victims of the shooting at Pulse Nightclub in Orlando, Florida on June 11, 2016.

The band joined forces with VH1 Save The Music, Toyota Giving and Life Is Beautiful. These organizations awarded three Las Vegas schools with a $40,000 **music education** grant to further music programs and fund new instruments. The band performed on September 21, 2017, at the Ed W. Clark High School for students and teachers to support this cause.

Imagine Dragons also supports **Musicians On Call**. This organization brings live and recorded music to bedsides of patients in healthcare facilities. By delivering live, in-room performances to patients undergoing treatment or unable to leave their beds, they add a dose of joy to the lives of the patients. The band has performed several shows in various healthcare facilities.

The band ended their almost 3 year hiatus with a great live performance at the **KultureBall 2021**. Daniel Platzman and Ben McKee are board members of KultureCity. This non-profit charity holds the KultureBall every year. KultureCity is the nations leading organization on sensory accessibility and acceptance for those with invisible disabilities.

In 2021, the band partnered with Walmart and posted an announcement on the platform TikTok. To **support and appreciate teachers**, Imagine Dragons gave a $5,000 gift card to 100 teachers which were nominated by their students on TikTok.

On March 27, 2022, the band were part of a charity event to end the war in Europe. The **"Save Ukraine - #Stop War"** event included more than 50 guests including Sting, Fatboy Slim, Bastille and many more.

Imagine Dragons did a video chat with Ukrainian president Zelensky in July 2022. Afterwards, they announced that they will be ambassadors for **U24**, an initiative which focuses on raising awareness and medical aid for the people of Ukraine.

Easter Eggs

SPOILER ALERT!!

Some easter eggs have been hidden in Imagine Dragons videos. Here are a few of them. But we will not mention every hidden secret 😈 Have fun discovering the rest!

On Top Of The World

One of the words that appears pretty often is the word SNOGARD. This is just DRAGONS spelt backwards.

There are several hidden references about director Stanley Kubrick´s work. The kid on the Bobby car at the very beginning represents Danny, a character from Kubricks film, The Shining. The model of the TV, that appears a few times in the video, is Monolith, a reference to 2001, another film by Stanley Kubrick. Interestingly enough, the number on Dan´s house in the video is 2001. Written on the hippie bus are the words Strange Love referencing Dr. Strangelove, again a film by Mr. Kubrick.

Matt Eastin (director) and Corey Fox (Co-director) made a cameo. In the video, Matt is sitting on the hood of the bus, Corey is the painter in the same scene. And Mac Reynolds is seated near the window.

Wayne´s car has a sticker on the window: Ragged Insomnia. It is an anagram for Imagine Dragons.

When Platz drives with his chopper, he passes by two road signs, Route 237 and Scenic Overlook. Both refer to Kubricks film The Shining. Room 237 is located at Overlook Hotel which is quite an important setting in the movie.

The crosswalk scene looks like The Beatles Abbey Road album. Some people believe in the conspiracy theory, that Paul McCartney died in 1966 and has been replaced with an imposter. In the music video, Ben is walking in Paul McCartneys spot without shoes (for some people a sign that he is dead) and as he passes the license plate of his car, it suddenly changes to „Paul is dead".

When the girls run through the security camera, the time code indicates 238,900 for a few frames... that's exactly the distance in miles from earth to the moon.

Whatever It Takes

In the video, there is a matchbook with the print „Mt. Qualo Colorado 80305". When you call the phone # on it, Dan picks up and tells you, „Whatever it takes. Go to". Then another band member (people assumed it was Ben) continues, „first line dot com". Sadly, this website doesn't exist anymore, but is was possible to go to fallingtoofasttoprepareforthis.com to get a sneak peak of the album „Evolve". (By the way: Colorado 80305 is the address of Shining Mountain...).

There were quite a few references back to the „On Top Of The World" video. Apart from the matchbook with the address of „Overlook Hotel", a picture with a rocket launch, a photo of Paul McCartney, and also the Scenic Overlook sign were shown in the video.

There was a sculpture of a boxing glove (for Believer) sinking in the water with the letters, Angora Man 9-4-12. Angora Man is an anagram for „no anagram" and Imagine Dragons album „Night Visions" was released on September 4, 2012.

The book titles in the underwater scenes are anagrams for the band members names.

A key is floating in the water which was a reference to the Radioactive music video.

Also in the underwater scene, there´s a license plate next to Ben. It says „A Demon is raging" which is an anagram for Imagine Dragons.

All the tokens and playing cards are of course a reference to the bands home town, Las Vegas.

Cutthroat

Right in the first few minutes, a sign appears in the video about „West Coast" DMV which obviously refers to the song from Origins.

On the counter of the DMV stands an award for „Gold standard in customer service". That´s a nice hint to the song Gold from the album Smoke + Mirrors.

„Please take a number" is a reference to the lyrics of Thunder.

Do the posters on the wall look familiar? Of course! They are screenshots of the On Top Of The World music video.

The license plate on the driving school car shows CT - THRT (Cutthroat), and the car air freshener as well as the fingernails of actress, Olivia Munn, feature the album cover of the Follow you/Cutthroat single.

On the globe which is situated on the counter of the DMV, stands a tiny human, which is a reference to „On Top Of The World".

And of course there´s also an anagram of Imagine Dragons again: Have a look at the drivers license: Dagger Insomnia.

They just love to tease their fans...

We'd like to give you an example how they love to interact with their fans. Let's have a closer look at the promotion for Mercury Act 1. To get access to a secret section on ID´s website, a password is required. To get this, you have to solve quests:

Suddenly, a song by „Ragged Insomnia" (an anagram for Imagine Dragons) appeared on various platforms. The title of the song is **Imagine Dragons**. You can hear the hint „Hopeless Opus backwards" when you play the song in reverse. If you listen to Hopeless Opus backwards, you can hear Dan singing „There is an anagram."

A video with the username There is an anagram was posted on Youtube. It was a song snippet from Mercury Act 1 called **Easy Come, Easy Go**. In the video were letters hidden. BG, DH, CC, FC. Converting them into numbers: 27.38, 33.64 and putting these coordinates into maps, it leads to a place called: Desert Breath, which in an aerial view looks like the solar system.

In the Easy Come, Easy Go video was also the symbol for the social media platform Facebook hidden („f"). So, after typing in „Desert Breath" on Facebook a new song appeared: **My Life,** which is another song snippet from their latest album.

The My Life video contained a lyric part, saying You´ve got to live your life. This is taken from the Night Visions song Cha-Ching. There is also a clock shown in the video which is ticking backwards. This led to the platform TikTok. After searching for the song title backwards (Gnihcahc), another new song snippet was revealed, **Lonely.**

In this video, you can see a bird and the text: „secondo album". This is obviously Italian, so after translating their second album title Smoke + Mirrors into Italian, you get: Fumo e specchi. And this username on Twitter has one video posted: the song #1. The video which is posted along with the song by this user is an autostereogram, like one of Imagine Dragons first EP´s. After having a closer look, the Discord symbol appeared.

ID created their own channel on Discord and posted that more clues are coming soon. They were surprised how fast everything was solved and Dan even talked to a few fans.

ID on Twitter

Imagine Dragons´s funniest, most
dramatic, serious und exciting tweets.

„I was just asked by the U.S.border patrol to please button up my pants."
#alltimelow May 25, 2013 Wayne Sermon

„Ben was telling me about the time, he had a 105 degree fever and almost died. Intense." Jul 28, 2013 Wayne Sermon (105 degree Fahrenheit = 40,6 degree Celsius)

„Holy shit. We won a Grammy."
Jan 27, 2014 Ben McKee

„Our driver thought our name was Dragonslayer. Should we change our name?"
Jan 27, 2014 Wayne Sermon

„Does anybody know where we can get a hurdy-gurdy and some highland bag pipes in Vegas ASAP? I love spontaneous inspiration in the studio."
Sep 4, 2014 Ben McKee

„Fried chicken right before a show isnt´t the BEST idea."
Feb 24, 2015 Wayne Sermon

„About once in a week, I get called „ma'am" by a stewardess or waiter walking behind me, but they always feel so awkward after, it's hilarious."
Mar 30, 2015 Wayne Sermon

„StilstuckonaplaneStillstuckonaplaneStillstuckonaplaneStillstuckonaplaneStillstuckonaplaneStillstuckonaplaneStillstuckonaplaneStilltuckonaplane."
Apr 25, 2015 Wayne Sermon

„Be a powerful human being. See everyone as yourself. A human being searching for peace in what can be a very difficult and confusing life."
Jun 1, 2015 Dan Reynolds

„I´m sick. Anyone have a puppy I can hold?“
Jul 4, 2015 Wayne Sermon

„Ben´s favorite candy bar is „Hershey's“ milk chocolate bar. If you're standing on his side of the stage, you should throw them to him!!“
July 25, 2015 Wayne Sermon

„Fill your pockets with mayonnaise packets and write your handle on it, then throw them at @wayneSermon on stage and he will follow you!“
Jul 25, 2015 Ben McKee

„Don´t grow up. It's a trap“ ;-)
Sep 8, 2015 Wayne Sermon

„We´re all just about 3 1/2 genes away from being a rice plant. So be grateful for what you got. ´Cause at least you're not rice.“ #grateful
Oct 15, 2015 Ben McKee

„Just can't stop thinking about @benamckee lately. His eyes. His arms. His hands....“ #mamcrushmonday #sexiestbassistever
Nov 23, 2015 Wayne Sermon

„Bella Terra movie theater in Huntington Beach, CA. At 7:30. Smoke and Mirrors movie. Come watch me watch myself, it'll be totes awkward.“
May 2, 2016 Wayne Sermon

Q&A with Wayne. „When you eat a taco, do you turn your head or the taco?“ Wayne replied: „I turn. You must always respect the taco. The taco was here long here before I was. You dig?“
Nov 28, 2016 Wayne Sermon

„If cookies were for dessert, and cookies were not finished, cookies WILL be for breakfast.“ #truth #alsotrueforpie
Dec 22nd, 2016 Ben McKee

„6 years ago I sold this guitar to buy a wedding ring. I'm randomly searching guitars, and here it is. In Korea!!?“
Apr 8, 2017 Wayne Sermon

„32 is the new 65. Who wants to play some bridge and go to bed early?“ #ormaybeagameofdominoes #olderequalswiser #longday #deepthoughtswithben Apr 30, 2017 Ben McKee

„For all the best song leaks, follow me! ;) “
Jun 13, 2017 Ben McKee

„HELP!!! WE DIDN´T GROW MUSTACHES!!! WE´VE BEEN REPLACED BY THE EVIL VERSIONS OF OURSELVES FROM MUSTACHE UNIVERSE!!! ALBUM TOMORROW!!!"
Jun 22, 2017 Ben McKee

„Happy Independence Day! Hey, artistic fans! How about some fan art of Wayne being attacked by a patriotic monkey?" #wayneisterrifiedofmonkeys.
Jul 4, 2017 Ben McKee

„BENNNNNNNNNNNNNNNNNNNNN"
Jul 4, 2017 Wayne Sermon

„Wayne is a sleepy panda
He tries as hard as he can-da
But when promo is early
He gets a bit surly
And rests his sad face on his hand-a"
Jul 6, 2017 Ben McKee

„Ben isn't in right now. If you'd like to leave a message, please do so after the beep. Beeeeeeeeep."
Jul 20, 2017 Ben McKee

„We are lucky. We are here because of you. We do this for YOU. Let us evolve together." Aug 12, 2017 Imagine Dragons

„Big announcement coming #soon..." (soon = days, not weeks)
Sep 14, 2017 Imagine Dragons

„Love us or hate us we are here to stayyyyyy mahahahahaha"
Nov 5, 2017 Imagine Dragons

„Holy Sound Check Batman!"
Feb 16, 2018 Daniel Platzman

„Is it possible to play a show after eating 4 pounds of JJJJ Jamon? Let´s find out!"
Apr 9, 2018 Imagine Dragons

„Imagine Dragons is meant to be a place of refuge. A place of safety. For all people. A place you can be you unabashedly. It´s meant to be a culture. A state of ambivalence to the world and its judging eyes. May it be a place of shelter. That´s all I want."
May 9, 2018 Dan Reynolds

„There are some mistakes that you can only appreciate when you get older.
For instance: In middle school my aol instant messenger screen name was „dandaladiesman“ - Needless to say I didn't have a single girlfriend in middle school.
Sometimes, u have to learn things the hard way.
And then I named my band Imagine Dragons.
Sometimes you never learn.“
May 11, 2018 Dan Reynolds

„Still jet lagged, but I did get to see penguins last night and I´m still giddy happy from seeing their cute little waddling“ #penguins
May 14, 2018 Daniel Platzman

„I've said the word „Thunder“ at least 50 million trillion billion times this year“
May 23, 2018 Imagine Dragons

„Confession: I´m actually terrified of confetti. Every night on stage I spend half of the time terrified and attempting to outrun an enemy who swarms about me coldly and without compassion. Come to the show. Watch the fun“
Jun 17, 2018 Ben McKee.

„Kitty Cat Ben´s favorite song to play live? „Meowth of the River“ of course!“
Jun 22, 2018 Ben McKee

„I can't tell you how many people thought it was ridiculous when I told them I was going to start a band in college. And now here I am.
Being a „realist“ is silly. You never make it to the stars without shooting for them and dreaming big.“
Jul 6, 2018 Dan Reynolds

„Waking up with that „holy crap I´m playing Red Rocks today“ feeling in my stomach“ #grateful #IsThisRealLife #3rdTimesACharm
Jul 16, 2018 Daniel Platzman

„As of today I officially announce that our band is neither a „pop band“ or „rock band“ Our genre is „I do what I want“
Thanks guys!“
Aug 3, 2018 Dan Reynolds

„And if they hate you. It´s ok. Believe in YOUR vision. Believe in you. Forget the rest. It´s just noise.“
Date unknown, Dan Reynolds

„That's the last time I ever make a joke about being in the illuminati
I got cousins calling me to check on me
The earth is flat sounds more convincing to me than the illuminati so I
thought I could joke about it. Wrong.
Next headline: „Dan Reynolds says earth is flat.“
Aug 3, 2018 Dan Reynolds

„We played in Alabama tonight & a fan threw a Rainbow flag on stage &
as I sang & looked at it on the ground I thought to myself, this is one of
the most conservative places we will play in America - if I pick that flag
up some fans will be upset - that's why I knew I HAD to pick it up.“
Aug 8, 2018 Dan Reynolds

„Only give love. Anything else is useless energy spent“
Aug 11, 2018 Dan Reynolds

„I've lived enough of my life remaining silent on these {LGTBQ} issues
because of fear or lack of education.
I don´t live in fear anymore.
I still have lots to learn. But no. I will be not be a silent voice with this
platform I have been given.“
Sep 2, 2018 Dan Reynolds

„We were never a cover band. Ever. Period. We played them on the side
to support our music. Tell your friends“ @Variety
Sep 27, 2018 Wayne Sermon

„But why ever shower if I can just put on more deodorant“
Oct 9, 2018 Dan Reynolds

Plane taking off. Man next to me asking if I´m ok cause I think I didn't
realize I was so worked up I was breathing heavy w a stern brow. Haha.
I gave him a big smile. „Oh me??? Yes of course!!“
„Wait you the radioactive guy?“
Sheeeeeeit.
Nov 11, 2018 Dan Reynolds

„Damn. I just really love you guys.“
Jan 14, 2019 Dan Reynolds

„We shouldn't hide behind a wall of dishonest perfection. It is truly
our struggles that makes us beautiful, resilent & beautifully
imperfect.“
Date unknown, Dan Reynolds

„We are having a baby boyyyyyy October 10th
@RealAjaVolkman I´m sorry I was 10lbs at birth I´m sorry“
Apr 4, 2019 Dan Reynolds

„New official least favorite-thing to do:
Applying eyedrops to a kitty Ow“
May 10, 2019 Daniel Platzman

„10 years and 3 days ago, @imaginedragons had our first rehearsal in
Vegas. Tonight we play to the biggest audience we have ever performed
for at the @ChampionsLeague opening ceremony in Madrid. We've
come a long way in the last decade. I love my band mates. I´m proud of
us all.“
Jun 1, 2019 BenMcKee

„I´ve been awake for too many hours“
Jun 6, 2019 Daniel Platzman

„Every day I choose to live because life is worth living! I accept my
depression and anxiety. I see it as my lifelong battle. It will never
get the best of me. For those of you who wake up feeling numb and
grey a lot of days - I know you - I AM you. Choose to stay alive w
me.“
Date unknown, Dan Reynolds

„We filmed our „Radioactive“ video 7 years ago in NY as Hurricane
Sandy started to make landfall. It was the first time meeting
@AADaddario and @LouDPhilips. None of us expected in our wildest
dreams that the video would be seen 1 BILLION times. Insane.“
Sep 4, 2019 Imagine Dragons

„Sauvignon blanc and Oreos do NOT mix“
Nov 28, 2019 Daniel Platzman

„Nothing Left To Say“ came out on our first album Night Visions almost
8 years ago. Cant believe its been so long. We fell in love with this video
made by some of our friends in France and wanted to share it with all of
you:
„Nothing left to say“ (Art film)"
Jan 20, 2020 Imagine Dragons

„Started wearing a cowboy hat in isolation to feel more brave. Totally
working“
Mar 29, 2020 Daniel Platzman

„It's Monday, time to set some goals for the week and smash ´em!"
May 4, 2020 Daniel Platzman

„Just know, you do a hell of a lot more for me than I could ever do for you. I love you XXdr."
May 15, 2020 Dan Reynolds

„Actually I'll probably be an aardvark in the next life not a Swan. Just a guess."
Jun 25, 2020 Dan Reynolds

„Imagine Dragons is not a band. It is a feeling of hope, happiness, sadness and vulnerability. It isn't a face or person. It is an emotion that resonates in your ear and spirit."
Aug 18, 2020 Dan Reynolds

„Happy birthday to the album that started it all. #nightvisions"
Sept 4, 2020 Imagine Dragons

„11 years ago today, we got to play a small side stage at the #biteoflasvegas festival after winning a battle of the bands. Pat Monahan (@train) got sick and we were asked to step in at the last second to perform to 20k people on the main stage. Sending love to our home town Vegas"
Oct 17, 2020 Imagine Dragons

„Some people call Ben´s voice „The Velvet Razor". It can only be safely observed from behind glass or after extensive audio processing."
Jun 14, 2021 Imagine Dragons

„IF ANYONE GUESSES THE ALBUM TITLE TONIGHT, WE WILL ANNOUNCE IT TOMORROW."
Jun 30, 2021 Imagine Dragons

„The answer was in the text. Look closer"
Jun 30, 2021 Imagine Dragons

„ok all. thank you. thank you thank you for all the kind words and warm reception to this record. It means so much to us all. You are the reason we do this. 10 years together. 10 more to come. You put a big smile on my face today for many many reasons. Love you all." XDR
Sept 4, 2021 Imagine Dragons

„Many of u have been asking about our old EP´s, & if we´d ever release them. We heard u, and today we released 3 old EP´s w/a previously unreleased demo on each from the very beginning of ID.“
Oct 15, 2021 Imagine Dragons

„If we don´t come back, tell our moms we love them. At least it´s for a good cause.“ [last tweet before Dan and -Wayne started a zero gravity flight for TRF]
Nov 7, 2021 Imagine Dragons

„Head over to our @discord server at 3pm PT for a surprise“
Mar 9, 2022 Imagine Dragons

„I love music because it´s the only thing I know that transfers human emotions in a way that people who live completly different lives can connect.“
Date unknown, Dan Reynolds

Q&A on Twitter: „Lipa“ asked: What´s the most random thing you have ever did in a show?
Renewed my car registration. Xoxoxo Wayne
Jul 2, 2022 Wayne Sermon

„tour has been everything and more.
thank you for singing with me. mourning loss and celebrating life.
thank you for all the lovely birthday wishes.
I have so much love for all of you. I can't wait to add these new songs into the set list for the US tour starting in 2 weeks“
Jul 17, 2022 Dan Reynolds

This is the legendary Dragon Wagon
Imagine Dragons toured America's west coast in this modified airport transporter. This vehicle was a gift to the band from Wayne´s father.

We asked fans on social media to share their thoughts on their favorite band....

When and how did you become a fan of Imagine Dragons?

„In 2015, a friend made me listen to Radioactive because, according to her, I was going to like that song. And she was not mistaken. From that moment on, I stood by. I've got their music on the computer and in the car. My life was a before and after them. I adore them.

Their songs are stories that happen to all of us. Thats why we identify with them. And the values they promote are the same ones they taught us and the ones we want for our children. That's why I´m following them. That's why I adore them." Maria

„It's more than 7 years ago. My now ex boyfriend was like „you know Radioactive and It's time? Well, this band is coming to Prague! Let's go" We met them right in front of the venue, everything was perfect. They stole my heart. I was 15 and it was my first concert ever. Also I had a HUUUGE crush on Dan and I fainted right in front of him. Also I forgot how to speak English. It was awkward." Claire

„In 2012, I saw Glee covering It's Time and I just loved this song. Then I looked it up and ever since I was hooked. Saw them in a small venue for the first time in 2013. One of the best concerts I saw." Joke

What do you think is the difference between Imagine Dragons and other bands? Is there any difference at all? What makes them so special?

„Whenever I am listening to Imagine Dragons I never have to worry about being judged..." Phthalo

„The vulnerable and relatable lyrics, the catchy and addictive melodies and the willingness to experiment with different sounds and different genres." Ana Marta

„The way that they genuinely care about their fans, it's amazing to see if sometime you find them on street, airport or whatever they will stop to talk with you, they will make sure you're okay, you're calm, that you don't have to rush because they are not going anywhere until you're done." Bia

„I think that they pay a lot of attention to people's mental health and I don't see that with other artists." Kayleigh

„Every band member is a role model. They don´t just talk about how to improve things, they are living it actively. They spread the right values." Astrid

„No matter how serious the subject matter or what Dan is going through, he keeps it clean, poetic, and quotable." Marcella

„They put their hearts, souls, and emotions into their songs."
Morgan Lyn

„You listen to their music and you realize the amount of talent each one has." Abi

You gain one hour with each band member. How do you spend your time with Dan, Platz, Ben and Wayne? (Child-friendly answers only, please...)

„I just let them play music. The best way is at my wedding." Jan

„I would ask him (Dan) respectfully where he learned to twerk that good (if this one is too much i'm sorry)." Tecla

„If I met Ben or Platz I'd like to talk about what the band used to be like in their early days, like with their old videos and funny stories. I love those. I could listen to any of them talk forever."
Bessie

„Wayne: Seems like he loves books, so I want to talk about books, and hear him talk about his love to the books." Maricot

„With Ben I would love to go into nature. I think he really likes this. I would love to take a hike with him in Malibu. There are opportunities for wonderful hikes there. Along the way I would like to talk with him about healthy food, which is an important thing for me, but I think for him too." Monique

„I would spend one hour with Dan Reynolds asking what his inspiration is and how it came to be and ask him on tips for lyric writing." David

„About Platz I would invite him out for some good tacos and let him know how much a fan I am of him! I love how he plays every instrument and so well. His high voices during concerts while he plays one (or two) instruments all at the same time... Blows my mind." Abi

„I'd love to cook with Wayne - his dishes look incredible yummy and healthy." Astrid

„With Ben, I'd love to talk about his philanthropy and what he learned from doing #TodayIGive for a whole year. I've always admired this side of him." Ana Marta

Is there anything you would improve about the band? Or any advice you would like to give them?

„Go on and stay as you are!" Jan

„There isn't anything I'd want to improve about the band. I would just tell them to keep staying true to themselves and to pay no mind to naysayers. I think when an artist gets to be so loved and so hated at the same time is because they're doing it right."
Ana Marta

„I would like for them to do more Collabs with well-known artist maybe one with Twenty One Pilots or maybe one with Panic! At The Disco or even Billie Eilish just to see how it sounds together. I think their sound is unique and I wouldn't want them to change anything about it unless they are trying something new with their own twist." David

„Not an improvement, just one advice that it's not actually for the band but for their team WE NEED MORE PICTURES OF PLATZ! Besides that I hope they never change who they really are." Bia

„Nothing needs to be improved! Imagine Dragons are those who they are — musicians without labels and pride. The only advice I could give them is just do what you like. Keep going guys!" Polina

„I really like the Rick Rubin influence; more of that quirky retro style would be fun down the road. But mostly I want them to be themselves and let us share their stories in whatever way they think is best. Don't ever do something just to be popular. The fans are loyal and the rest will follow." Marcella

Was there anything special about the band that you would like to share?

„Back in November 2018, they came to a concert here in Monterrey, México. I was very excited, I laughed, cried and sang all the songs. It was a great concert.

Then "Demons" started and at the half Dan said some really thoughtful words about mental health and it touched me. A month later I was diagnosed and if I ever have the chance I would thank him for that." Abi

„Imagine Dragons makes music about serious issues like self doubt, pain and triumph, facing your fears. Such depth of thought is rarely found on the shallow surface of automated playlists and run-of-the-mill radio stations, which is what most people end up building their personal taste off of. And yet there Imagine Dragons is on that surface: you don't have to dig to discover them, yet they beckon you to go further." Marcella

„Some songs can really cheer me up, and some songs put my feet back on the ground. Other songs make me think again. That's very special when you can achieve that as a band. Also what you are doing with TRF and LoveLoud, that means so much. You can be so very proud of yourselves. I can only thank you." Monique

„It's Time helped me though a difficult time when some of my family members didn't accept me because I'm gay. A lot of their songs are like an escape for me and when I listen to them I feel happy and safe." Alli

„Thanks to Dan for all those kind words he says every concert, thanks to Platz because of whom I started playing drums, thanks to Wayne for these amazing guitar solos and who has taught me how to work hard, and thanks to Ben who's the kindest person I've ever known. Imagine Dragons music is my inspiration." Polina

„Being their fan for 10 years now has changed me, since I was a teenager being bullied in high school and only having them or people I've meet on Twitter (because of them) as my friends, to being a married woman with real life responsibilities, to being a divorced woman rediscovering life and finding happiness again... They have been with me during all that, they don't know any of this, but they have been with me all along!" Bia

„I only became a fan in 2021, shortly after the release of "Follow You" and "Cutthroat". However, they came into my life just when I needed them the most. The summer of 2021 was a very confusing and challenging time. The song "It's Time" made me feel like it wasn't right to leave college when I was about to do it. Thankfully, I didn't give the Academy a rain check. How ironic! Also, "Whatever It Takes" gave me encouragement at a time where no one believed in my abilities. I could never thank Imagine Dragons enough for being there for me when no one else was. I'll be forever in debt."
Ana Marta

„The album Smoke + Mirrors, this one helped me so much when my grandpa passed away. The week of the funeral, I blasted this as loud as possible, at home or in the car or in my headphones. When the song Dream came on, I realized how much of a dream life basically was to me at that moment (more a nightmare). I saw my grandpa, and I still couldn't believe it was him, that everything we went through was gone. Everything was just one big memory from that moment on. So the whole week, I kept listening to the album, and especially to the song Dream. And I don't know how to say it right, but it relieved me, it made me feel like as if I had a weight on my shoulder being gone. I felt so much strength in it. And if I ever get the chance to thank them for this, I would love to do that. (if I am not too shy then)" Tecla

„I would like to share my love for the song Selene. It has pushed me through my darkest times and it always helps me calm down. I love it with all my heart and hopefully, one day I'll get to hear it live" :) Phtahlo

Sadness is my enemy
I fear time will age him gently
Walkin´ by my side for all these years
Seems that we´ve grown friendly
Happiness is beautiful to see
Won´t you box it up for me?

Burn Out
Origins

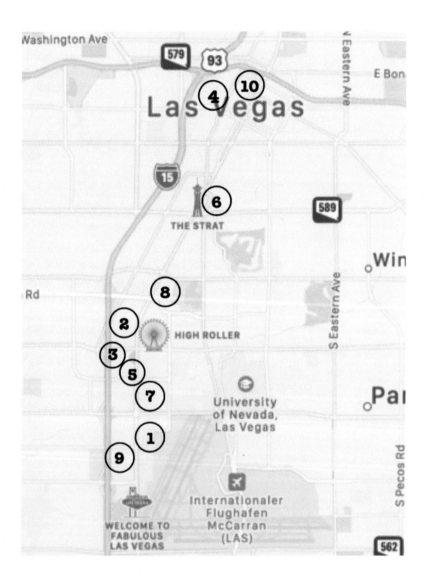

01 **„Vegas Strong" Benefit concert**
All proceeds of this performance went directly to the victims of the mass shooting from October 1, 2017. On this day, an assassin shot more than 1000 bullets from the 32 floor of the Mandalay Bay hotel towards the visitors of a local music festival (Route 91 Harvest Festival). Sixty people died at this cruel shooting and more than 800 visitors were hurt.

02 **O´Shea´s Casino**
Ben´s face was licked by a fan at this location. This was a hoax from Dan. You can find more information about this incident in the category „Little Known Facts About Imagine Dragons".

03 **Bellagio**
The video for „Whatever It Takes" was filmed at the Bellagio, which is famous for their water fountains.

04 **Fremont Street**
The band performed their song "Shots" here during the commercial break of the Grammy Awards. Imagine Dragons were the first band ever to do this kind of performance. Please have a look at the chapter Promotion of Smoke + Mirrors to read more about this legendary live performance.

05 **The Cosmopolitan**
The Origins Experience took place at this beautiful location. It was the official launch of ID´s fourth album, Origins. The release show was a mixture of live performance and awards ceremony. The band shed a light on several people who stood by their side from the very beginning. And they also performed their older songs as well as new ones from Origins.

06 **The STRAT**
The video for "Shots - (Broiler Remix)" was filmed here.

07 **The Joint** (Hard Rock Casino)
The music video for one of Imagine Dragons´ most famous songs, Demons, was filmed at this location.

08 **Wynn**
The last TRF Gala (2021) took place in this hotel.

09 **House of Blues**
ID had their first gigs at this venue as a young, unsigned band.

10 **Bite of Las Vegas Festival**
The band's first performance in front of more than 20.000 people who attended this festival.

Music & Monsters

Sitting
Too still
Tick, tock, goes the clock
Around and again spins my brain
They're here
Haunting me, creeping inside me
Screaming too loud for me to block them out
I take a deep breath
Lay down on the icy floor
My fingers tremble as I slide on the headphones
Squeeze my eyes shut, wait
Just a little longer—

Floor falls away beneath my feet
I'm falling, and it's okay
I'm falling, and I'm escaping
I land in a new place

There are lights in this place
They flicker and flash, faster and faster
Stabbing through my eyes
Shining down on me
Showering me in their glory
I take it in, and I hold it close

Steady beat
Snapping, cracking, hissing
BANG BANG BANG
Thump thump thump
It throbs with my pulse until we're one
Tap my foot against the ground
Bounce with the rhythm, I'm weightless
It fills me with that power
Power that is mine

Sweet, silky notes glide through the air
And I fly with them
They surround me; they fill me
I know them, and I follow them
Let them lead me through this place
Guide me through this labyrinth of sound
I'm getting closer
It's heavy, it's strong, it's steady
Echoing in my blood
Words that pound in my mind
Words that fall from my lips
Words that sink down into my core
I soak them up, let them shield me
They become a part of me
And now I'm here

Monsters stand in front of me
Eyes glowing, teeth glistening
Claws outstretched, ready to tear me to pieces
They hover above me, blocking out the light
Force me into that dark place again
The place where I'm alone
Where tears drip down my face, I shake, and I'm scared
But I won't stay here this time

I feel it rising
The melody, it charges my soul
Waiting, waiting, waiting
Take a deep breath as it builds
Explosion of sound, fire in the air

I'm alive, do you hear me?
I'm alive, and I'm taking back my soul
I don't need a weapon
I have myself, and I am strong

Stare down the monsters, make them cower in the corner
I AM ALIVE, AND YOU CAN'T HURT ME ANYMORE

As the music erupts into sparks around me
I fly, I dance, and I lift my head
The light shines down on me once more
I smile
I'm free

Snap
It crumbles to pieces
I'm sitting on my floor once more
Mouthing lyrics
Feet and fingers tapping to the beat
I feel it in my body; the words swarm inside me
The last sparkling notes and—
Silence

Open my eyes, wince because this world is too bright
I sigh and take off the headphones
Sit up and look around
Smile, just a little
And I go slay my monsters

I smile all day, and cry through the night
Won´t someone please save my
Life is fleeting
Dull Knives taking my life
A slow burn fire from the inside
Dull Knives twisting my spine

Dull Knives
Mercury Act 1 & 2

Insider - Knowledge for Firebreathers

lead poisoning @dan

Wayne's tourbus cooking
@evolve tour

"CAB"

#kittycatdance

DIRTY DOGS

"So, are you guys famous?"

Britney Spears

#asksofthands

Ragged Insomnia

#flyku

DANRANGE

Aquavit @ben

#curlyfrieshair

"Radioactive guy"

#SOON

Dan ties his shoes
on stage - almost in
every show

RIP Dan's pants Paris + Las Vegas 2017

Illuminati

Vlog

MYSPACE

How'd the chicken get in there?

Blonde hair Dan

Tarantula in the Donut box

Banangie

Dragonwagon

Dandaladiesman

BEAT BOXING

♪ Where Matt
Damon hides... ♪

Evil Mustache Ben #EvilBenmckee

Hershey's milk chocolate bar @ben

#Danforgotthemilk

Destination Dragons Tour

Legendary performance @platz Karaoke, Manila

#DEGG

Lead poisoning Dan:
Because he was hungry and the milk wasn't cold enough for a yummy cereal meal, Dan decided to put ice packs into his bowl. It worked, but, after finishing his meal, he discovered weird dark spots on the bottom of his bowl. He was concerned that the ice packs were broken and he would get lead poisoning. He googled it and discovered later that the mysterious spots were only chocolate chips from his cereal.

Wayne´s tourbus cooking @Evolve tour:
During the Evolve tour, Wayne and his wife, Alex, used to do short videos showing them preparing their tour meals.

„CAB":
Mac was texting the band and asked them, if they „Cab be at .... In an hour". It was a simple typo, but the guys made fun of that for quite long time by replying: „I don´t know.. cab we?.." „Cab you do this for us?"....

#kittycatdance:
The legendary performance of Ben McKee during various songs. His dance reminiscent of a cat hitting something with its paws.Ben performed it mostly during the songs Yesterday and Mouth Of The River.

Dirty Dogs:
This term is about their performance after diving in mud due to severe weather at the Glastonbury Festival in Great Britain. It has also been used (mostly by Dan) as a playful insult for the other band members. It is still used in the flamily (another term for the ID fandom).

„So, are you guys famous?":
This was once asked by a lady selling fruit juice at a stand in Asia. Platz was so surprised by her question, that he accidentally spit the juice on her and the incident was very embarrassing for him.

Britney Spears:
When ID first started performing, they played half the set using cover songs and half of their own creations. Many of the cover songs were from Britney Spears.

#flyku:
This hashtag has been used many times by Platz when he posted pictures which he had taken from a plane while flying.
It´s origins are in Haiku, which is a type of poetry originating in Japan.

#asksofthands:
Ben has done quite a few Q&A sessions. He asked the fandom to use this hashtag when asking him something.

Danrange:
A fun orange juice brand that was invented in the fandom after Dan ate an orange in the Next To Me music video. „Danrange" became so popular that it has its own Twitter page and also seen by the band.

Ragged Insomnia:
Imagine Dragons is, according to the band, an anagram. Many people believe, the correct name of the band is Ragged Insomnia. It is such a popular theory, that even the band used it as an Easter egg in their videos of On Top Of The World and Whatever It Takes.

Aquavit @Ben:
Ben had a bad experience during their stay in Norway. He drank too much Aquavit (an alcohol spirit) and therefore he couldn't remember much of what happened afterwards.

#curlyfrieshair:
This was Dan´s nickname during the Smoke + Mirrors era.

„Radioactive guy":
Dan traveled on a plane and was recognized by a guy who addressed him as „Radioactive guy", and this term stuck.

#soon:
It is known in the fandom, that when the band or one of its members uses „soon", it means some point in time between one day and one year... or even longer.

Dan ties his shoes on stage:
It seems like Dan has loose shoelaces at literally every show. Now it is a running joke that he needs to tie his shoes at almost every show.

RIP Dan´s pants Paris + Las Vegas 2017:
During Dan´s performance at Lollapalloza in Paris he tore his pants. The same happened at a charity event (Vegas Strong) in Las Vegas. For both events are videos on YouTube available...

Illuminati:
Dan thought it would be funny to do a series of short videos on Twitter which indicated he was a member/insider of the secret organization, The Illuminati. After a few people took it very seriously, he even had to do a withdrawal tweet...

How'd the chicken get in there?:
Mac, Imagine Dragons manager tweeted, and somehow an emoji of a chicken appeared in the tweet. He was very confused and tweeted this legendary sentence, which is still used in the fandom: How did the chicken get in there??

Vlog:
At the beginning of ID´s career, the band used to make Vlog entries. It was kind of a video diary and it documented their daily lives.

Footprints:
This is a hint for Dan´s well known dislike of feet.

Banangie:
This term was introduced during the Smoke +. Mirrors tour (North American Leg). Ben and Platz had fun taking a banana with a painted lady face to photoshoots and meet & greets. It was named after Angie Warner, their tour manager (and Mother of Dragons) during ID´s Smoke + Mirrors Tour. Banangie made a brief cameo at Ben´s cooking contribution for TRF in May 2020.

Blonde hair Dan:
Dan had blonde dyed hair for a short period of time

MySpace:
Confession: Yes, the band also had a MySpace page.

Tarantula in Donut Box:
The band pranked their sound engineer with a living spider in a donut box. They chased the poor guy through the whole studio with the tarantula. This happened at the recording session for Night Visions.

Handcuffs:
Ben had once been arrested for public indecency and Dan had to get him out of prison for a performance.

Dragonwagon:
This is the legendary tour bus of Imagine Dragons.

Dandaladiesman:
Dan´s instant messenger username in middle school. Hm, choosing this nickname wasn't his best decision...

Beat Boxing:
Dan can beatbox... he showed this skill at LoveLoud 2019.

„Where Matt Damon hides“:
It´s a listening mistake.. a few people hear in the song Demons „Where Matt Damon hides“.

Evil Mustache Ben #Evil Benmckee:
During the Evolve era, the whole band grew mustaches and Ben had the theory that Mustache-Ben would be his evil alter ego.

Hershey´s Milk Chocolate Bar @Ben:
This is a prank between Ben and Wayne. Knowing that Ben dislikes this kind of chocolate, Wayne tweeted several times that fans should throw Hershey bars to Ben, he would appreciate it. Of course the fans complied with this request and gave Ben his „favorite“ chocolate at a concert in Seoul (August 2015). Ben then reciprocated by tweeting, Wayne would love to get little packs of mayonnaise, and we are pretty sure, mayonnaise isn't Wayne´s favorite food.

#Danforgotthemilk:

A firebreather started this hashtag, just for fun. It´s been added to a lot of tweets - for example when a band member looked at Dan with a weird facial expression: #Danforgotthemilk.

Destination Dragons Tour:

As part of the promotion for their album, Smoke + Mirrors, Imagine Dragons did a mini tour where they performed at small clubs. Those clubs were ones in which the band played their first gigs. Flying from Los Angeles to Salt Lake City, Las Vegas and finally to Atlanta the band even performed in the plane for their fans!

Legendary performance @platz Karaoke, Manila:

Platz couldn't resist doing a small karaoke performance while they were visiting the Philippines. His rendition of Queen's Bohemian Rhapsody has become legendary.

#DEGG:

Is a common saying in the fandom to describe something weird, embarrassing or a failure. It´s origin is a picture of Dan with Tyler Glenn. Dan said he looked kinda weird on the photo. So the fans took it and turned it into this meme. #DEGG was born.

Answers and References

Answers to the quiz:

Q1:   Yes, at the very beginning the band was named Lavender for a few weeks.

Q2:   Dan broke his hand in Berlin because he hit the big drum too hard while performing Radioactive.

Q3:   Wayne has a monkey phobia.

Q4:   Yes, they won a Grammy in 2014 for Radioactive in the category „Best Rock Performance".

Q5:   It was Platz that was asked last to join the band, Imagine Dragons.

Q6:   Platz and Ben have similar tattoos

Q7:   No. The music video for Believer features a boxing match, but it is between Dan Reynolds and Dolph Lundgren.

And these are the hidden words in the word searching game:

Radioactive, Its Time, Demons, On Top Of The World, Hear Me, Shots, I Bet My Life, Gold, Next To Me, Thunder, Whatever It Takes, Believer, Natural, Bad Liar, Zero, Birds, Machine, Cutthroat, Follow You, Wrecked, Monday, Bones, Sharks

Specials:

Evolve, Night Visions, Origins, Mercury, Platz, Dan, Wayne, Ben, Smoke, Mirrors, Guitar, Mic, Bass, Fun, Drums, Aja, Eastin, Love, Cat, Alex

What term does not fit in here:

Bleeding out - all other songs are from Smoke + Mirrors
Dog - all other terms are for Platz and he has a cat
Next to me - all other music videos were directed by Matt Eastin
Friction - all other songs are from Evolve
Valentine - all other kids are from Waynes Family
Ford Mustang - all other terms are for Wayne

Who was it?

1		W	A	M				
2	C	A	N	T	O	R		
3	T	Y	L	E	R			
4	E	N	E	M	Y			
5	B	E	L	L	A	G	I	O

Emoji Game

1) Smoke and Mirrors, 2) I Don´t Know Why, 3) Hear Me,
4) Every Night, 5) Dancing In The Dark, 6) The Fall,
7) Mouth Of The River, 8) On Top Of The World,
9) Bleeding Out, 10) Summer. 11) Love, 12) Nothing Left To Say
13) Digital, 14) Sharks, 15) West Coast, 16) Rise Up,
17) Burn Out, 18) Dolphins, 19) Bones, 20) Next To Me

www.celebrityborn.com,
https://www.mormonstories.org/podcast/wayne-and-alex-sermon-our-journey-with-imagine-dragons-and-mormonism/
www.gibson.com,
http://www.fasterlouder.com.au/features/36345/Imagine-Dragons-That-arena-sound-excites-us-we-dont-need-to-apologise-for-it#?oszDfaxPIuAwUX6.99,
https://web.archive.org/web/20140715001620/,
http://jammagazine.com/mf201302-imagine-dragons-its-time-interview-guitarist-wayne-sermon-writer-david-dunn.aspx#
https://variety.com/2020/dirt/entertainers/imagine-dragons-wayne-sermon-thunders-into-rolling-hills-ranch-1234715360/
https://www.mormonstories.org/podcast/wayne-and-alex-sermon-our-journey-with-imagine-dragons-and-mormonism/,
jammagazine.com.
https://imaginedragons.fandom.com/wiki/Wayne_Sermon,
https://ethnicelebs.com/wayne-sermon
https://www.bbc.com/news/entertainment-arts-40277696
https://www.dallasobserver.com/music/wayne-wing-sermon-of-imagine-dragons-on-being-a-mormon-rock-star-7059155,
https:www.youtube.com/watch?v=CwHBOJvXgUk,
https://utahvalley360.com/2018/03/04/2018-fab-40-jeff-sermon/
https://www.youtube.com/watch?v=PzWyyFCEhs0
https://atwoodmagazine.com/idev-imagine-dragons-2018-interview-evolve,
https://www.youtube.com/watch?v=tEgZWA1avVA
https://universe.byu.edu/2014/04/15/an-angel-amongst-dragons1/
https://www.youtube.com/watch?v=X4o2SXaDjiE
https://www.youtube.com/watch?v=hGDnHlFtl4U
https://www.youtube.com/results?search_query=wayne+sermon+mormon
https://www.youtube.com/watch?v=hPpkNOb_Gmc
American Fork Highschool Homepage
https://www.bonedo.de/artikel/einzelansicht/gear-chat-und-interview-mit-wayne-sermon-von-imagine-dragons.html
https://www.dallasobserver.com/music/wayne-wing-sermon-of-imagine-dragons-on-being-a-mormon-rock-star-7059155
 https://marriott.byu.edu/mpa/news/?article=675
https://vegasmagazine.com/wayne-sermon-talks-the-upcoming-st-judes-heart-of-fashion-gala
https://vimeo.com/342263563
https://vegasmagazine.com/wayne-sermon-talks-the-upcoming-st-judes-heart-of-fashion-gala
Imagine Dragons - Live Nation
https://www.youtube.com/watch?v=PatM6hWdI_g
https://www.youtube.com/watch?v=LtIZ3U2l0CI
https://en.wikipedia.org/wiki/Daniel_Platzman,
https://www.imbued.com/name/nm3769549/bio?ref_=nm_ov_bio_sm,
https://www.drummersresource.com/daniel-platzman-imagine-dragons-interview,
https://medium.com/quickys/blackatpaideia-zoomer-activism-rattles-a-progressive-school-3d5f8bceec3c
https://www.youtube.com/watch?v=748nOTZZqQM
https://www.drummersresource.com/daniel-platzman-imagine-dragons-interview,
https://danielplatzman.com,
https://www.youtube.com/watch?app=desktop&v=LY7IBgOpNmQ&feature=youtu.be
https://www.youtube.com/watch?v=lpyOvLD1JDQ
https://vegasmagazine.com/digital-editions year 2015, issue 1, spring,
https://www.toyota-global.com/company/history_of_toyota/75years/vehicle_lineage/car/id60012328/index.html
https://www.youtube.com/watch?app=desktop&v=LY7IBgOpNmQ&feature=youtu.be
https://web.archive.org/web/20150720232658/,
http://www.drummagazine.com/features/post/daniel-platzman-dream-the-wildest-dreams
Booklet of Mercury Act 1
https://www.youtube.com/watch?v=PzWyyFCEhs0
https://genius.com/albums/Daniel-platzman/Carpe-diem-original-motion-picture-soundtrack
https://www.youtube.com/watch?v=LtIZ3U2l0CI
https://www.redbull.com/us-en/imagine-dragons-interview,
https://www.tnp.sg/entertainment/music/dragon-can-cook-rendang
https://atwoodmagazine.com/smoke-and-mirrors-conversation-imagine-dragons
https://www.youtube.com/watch?v=wwpxxIwupgk
https://www.amazon.de/Pun-Games-II-Electric-Boogaloo/dp/B00SFNQUNU/ref=sr_1_1?
__mk_de_DE=ÅMÅŽÕÑ&keywords=daniel+platzman+Pun+and+games+II&qid=1636825828&sr=8-1
https://www.imdb.com/title/tt1541723/fullcredits/?ref_=tt_ov_st_sm
https://goldminesaloon.net/platinum/multi-platinum-grammy-award-winning-band-imagine-dragons-to-perform-at-kultureball-2021-news/
https://www.kulturecity.org/meet-the-kulturciy-team,
Platzman´s Twitter Account, Tweet from 09.10.21
www.kulturecity.org
Interveiw with Daniel Platzman (Kulture City from May, 9th 2021
https://imaginedragons.home.blog/60-2/
https://www.youtube.com/watch?v=PzWyyFCEhs0
https://www.youtube.com/watch?v=RYbNW920kOs
https://www.youtube.com/watch?v=748nOTZZqQM
https://www.youtube.com/watch?v=qXsFNeReUms
https://www.youtube.com/watch?v=LtIZ3U2l0CI
https://www.imbd.com/title/tt541723/fullcredits/?ref_=tt_ov_st_sm,
https://www.imdb.com/name/nm4995251/?ref_=fn_al_nm_1
Twitter of Ben McKee June, 2nd 2021
https://www.berklee.edu/berklee-now/news/a-tough-year-inspired-imagine-dragons-ben-mckee-to-do-more-active-
https://imaginedragons.home.blog/60-2,
https://www.mormonstories.org/podcast/wayne-and-alex-sermon-our-journey-with-imagine-dragons-and-mormonism/,
https://imaginedragonsworld.com/imagine-dragons-talk/427-ben-mckee-apreciation-post.html,

https://www.youtube.com/watch?v=748nOTZZqQM
https://web.archive.org/web/20150923183710/
http://www.berkleegroove.com/2013/08/04/staff-pick-of-august-imagine-dragons-interview/
https://www.goldenplec.com/imagine-dragons-interview/
https://www.drummersresource.com/daniel-platzman-imagine-dragons-interview,
https://www.youtube.com/watch?v=dzufZOVKuPo
https://www.youtube.com/watch?v=upVbHKX2W40
https://www.youtube.com/watch?v=R2seLOdiZtk
https://www.youtube.com/watch?v=hgW9hXqIwg0
https://www.youtube.com/watch?v=R3_htbh_Jdw
https://www.redbull.com/us-en/imagine-dragons-interview,
https://www.youtube.com/watch?v=daTVvXxFJ50
https://www.youtube.com/watch?v=RYbNW920kOs
https://www.goldenplec.com/imagine-dragons-interview,
https://www.youtube.com/watch?v=X4o2SXaDjiE
https://imaginedragonsworld.com/imagine-dragons-talk/427-ben-mckee-appreciation-post,
https://ethnicelebs.com/daniel-platzman
https://goldminesaloon.net/platinum/multi-platinum-grammy-award-winning-band-imagine-dragons-to-perform-at-kultureball-2021-news/
https://ethnicelebs.com/ben-mckee
According to Ben´s Twitter post from January 5th 2022
https://www.thesunsetstrip.com/thesunsetstripcom-exclusive-interview-imagine-dragons/
https://wwww.pressdemocrat.com/article/entertainment/imagine-dragons-bass-player-road-from-forestville-to-bottlerock/?gallery=AE6E978C-7854-4EAC-B39B-3C76A2D8EE6F
Twitterfeed of Ben McKee from May 18th 2021
https://www.reddit.com/r/imaginedragons/comments/qr5g9q/were_imagine_dragons_and_were_neither_a/
According to his reply to a tweet on December 6, 2018
https://www.youtube.com/watch?v=PatM6hWdI_g
https://www.youtube.com/watch?v=748nOTZZqQM
https://www.youtube.com/watch?v=lpyOvLD1JDQ
https://www.youtube.com/watch?v=LtIZ3U2iOCI
https://www.youtube.com/watch?v=Y-kwuLNBPQs
https://www.billboard.com/articles/6472705/imagine-dragons-cover-smoke-and-mirrors-touring-grammys,
https://l.facebook.com/l.php?u=https%3A%2F%2F
https://www.usatoday.com/story/life/tv/2018/06/22/imagine-dragons-dan-reynolds-talks-mormon-faith-lgbtq-doc-believer/722517002fbclid=IwAR34KHbbqeeEFU_P4oiFK998TMHsptCEyULAk8DTaEPxQcKUgDMy2P6GiC4&h=ATO2hYmTWMpp4yx5ac9Ab6Xc_4pEiyWtKRfrDAVo119NOtIaSTxZ2n8t43ON1f9nfXZeKwD6s-R3e6zrgKJ_UDo2VHyf7RQb_U_ho20oT7Ne7NN3AFkPDhLUOtaIaBxpk7kDXGyq
https://twitter.com
https://www.youtube.com/watch?v=LObzpbvysds
https://www.kulturecity.org/meet-the-kulturcity-team
https://womensaudiomission.org
https://www.tmz.com/2019/08/19/imagine-dragons-ben-mckee-new-tattoo-cosmic-intelligence/
https://www.youtube.com/watch?v=gIxDEf2d1cA
https://www.timetoast.com/timelines/dan-reynolds
https://universe.byu.edu/2014/11/13/reynolds-success-its-all-in-the-family1/,
Dan Reynolds Plays Songs & Answers Questions | Instagram Live 4/5/20
https://www.independent.co.uk/arts-entertainment/music/features/imagine-dragons-interview-lyrically-it-most-raw-i-feel-very-timid-about-lot-material-10236448.html,
https://www.npr.org/2018/02/03/582833787/from-mormon-missionary-to-lgbtq-advocate-and-international-rock-star?t=1603443362400,
https://time.com/5322558/imagine-dragons-dan-reynolds-lgbtq/
https://knpr.org/knpr/2017-01/imagine-dragons-dan-reynolds-depression-deepest-when-bands-fame-grew,
https://www.sfexaminer.com/entertainment/imagine-dragons-on-musical-mission/?oid=2317034,
https://www.youtube.com/watch?v=dzufZOVKuPo
Instagram account Neale Hoerle
https://latterdaysaintmusicians.com/artists/dan-reynolds
https://people.com/music/imagine-dragons-dan-reynolds-on-chronic-disease/,
https://www.dailynews.com/2017/03/17/how-imagine-dragons-reynolds-is-fighting-back-against-as-diagnosis/,
https://vegasmagazine.com/digital-editions 2015 issue 1 spring
https://www.laweekly.com/imagine-dragons-dan-reynolds-and-nico-vegas-aja-volkman-reynolds-weirdly-perfect-romance/
https://www.billboard.com/articles/news/6472714/imagine-dragons-billboard-cover-sneak-peek,
https://www.youtube.com/watch?v=zA94a3re81w
Dan Reynolds Answers Fan Questions | Twitch Live 8/22/19,
https://people.com/music/dan-reynolds-wife-marriage-counseling-fight-for-family/,
http://www.nightlifebutler.com/las-vegas-event/body-english-nye-2014-party-ft-dan-reynolds/
https://people.com/parents/dan-reynolds-split-wife-aja-apocalypse-parents-interview/,
Live Chat with Dan on Youtube at the premiere of „Wrecked" mv on July 15th 2021
https://www.ktnv.com/news/imagine-dragons-frontman-dan-reynolds-donates-childhood-las-vegas-home-in-support-of-lgbtq-youth
LoveLoudfest.com
Interview with Executive Director Clarissa Savage from June, 6th 2021
https://www.billboard.com/articles/columns/rock/8239703/imagine-dragons-next-to-me-video-mini-movie
https://nypost.com/2018/11/08/imagine-dragons-singer-on-saving-marriage-and-lgbtq-kids/,
https://extratv.com/2019/04/03/dan-reynolds-and-aja-volkman-expecting-baby-boy-months-after-calling-off-divorce/,
tps://www.youtube.com/watch?v=YQWd3wd7GYE
https://eu.usatoday.com/story/entertainment/celebrities/2019/12/26/imagine-dragons-dan-reynolds-proposes-his-wife-again-after-split/2753989001/,
https://blog.scoutingmagazine.org/2014/04/08/imagine-dragons-lead-singer-dan-reynolds-is-an-eagle-scout/
https://metro.co.uk/2013/02/05/dan-reynolds-its-time-is-a-song-i-wrote-at-a-low-point-in-my-life-3380799/
https://www.dallasobserver.com/music/wayne-wing-sermon-of-imagine-dragons-on-being-a-mormon-rock-star-7059155,
https://www.usmagazine.com/celebrity-news/news/dan-reynolds-says-split-from-wife-made-them-stronger/
https://www.standard.co.uk/go/london/music/holy-roller-dan-reynolds-interview-8928525.html,
Dan Reynolds Answers Fan Questions | Twitch Live 8/22/19

Mercury Act 1 booklet
https://knpr.org/knpr/2017-01/imagine-dragons-dan-reynolds-depression-deepest-when-bands-fame-grew
https://web.archive.org/web/20150722094512/,
http://www.drummagazine.com/features/post/daniel-platzman-dream-the-wildest-dreams/P2/
https://www.youtube.com/watch?v=PzWyyFCEhs0,
Imagine Dragons - Interview at Virgin Radio 2017,
https://www.youtube.com/watch?v=hGDnHlFtl4U
https://www.youtube.com/watch?v=PatM6hWdI_g
Dan Reynolds talks about Origins Tour & singing, Instagram live
https://www.youtube.com/watch?v=Q7-yRMwopE0
https://variety.com/2020/dirt/entertainers/imagine-dragons-dan-reynolds-buys-goldie-hawns-former-malibu-beach-house-1234705339/
https://www.youtube.com/watch?v=qXsFNeReUms
https://genius.com/Steve-angello-someone-else-lyrics
https://www.youtube.com/watch?v=dzufZOVKuPo
https://www.billboard.com/articles/news/6133924/imagine-dragons-battle-cry-new-music-radioactive,
https://www.laweekly.com/imagine-dragons-dan-reynolds-and-nico-vegas-aja-volkman-reynolds-weirdly-perfect-romance/
https://www.youtube.com/watch?v=R3_htbh_Jdw
https://www.standard.co.uk/go/london/music/holy-roller-dan-reynolds-interview-8928525.html
https://illinoisentertainer.com/2015/02/cover-story-imagine-dragons/
https://podcasts.apple.com/at/podcast/001-dan-reynolds-imagine-dragons/id1405795796?i=1000415451286
https://genius.com/Imagine-dragons-so-many-voices-lyrics#about
https://www.youtube.com/watch?v=LtIZ3U2IOCI
https://presslasvegas.com/news/imagine-dragons-singer-makes-first-donation-at-summerlins-giving-machine/
http://www.nightstreetrecords.com,
https://www.bmi.com/news/entry imagine_dragons_dan_reynolds_to_be_honored_with_hal_david_starlight_award,
Dan Reynolds Plays Songs & Answers Questions | Instagram Live 4/5/20,,
https://www.imdb.com/title/tt7689424/?ref_=nv_sr_srsg_6
https://www.billboard.com/articles/6472705/imagine-dragons-cover-smoke-and-mirrors-touring-grammys
https://www.universal-music.de/yungblud/news/original-me-der-neue-song-von-yungblud-feat-dan-reynolds-256074,
https://variety.com/2020/music/news/tom-morello-imagine-dragons-dan-reynolds-stand-up-1234696896/#!
https://genius.com/Dan-reynolds-and-hans-zimmer-skipping-stones-lyrics
https://web.archive.org/web/20180612142734/https://loveloudfest.com/press-release,
https://universe.byu.edu/2017/08/23/loveloud-festival-gives-support-to-lgbtq-youth1/,
https://www.hbo.com/documentaries/believer/about,
https://www.dailynews.com/2017/03/17/how-imagine-dragons-reynolds-is-fighting-back-against-as-diagnosis/
https:// www.monsterpainintheas.co
https://www.goodmorningamerica.com/news/video/tim-cook-dan-reynolds-ryan-smith-team-support-76105908
https://utahvalley360.com/2013/12/27/15-things-you-didnt-know-about-imagine-dragons-on-top-of-the-world-video/
https://www.youtube.com/watch?v=YhhbD2d1mxA
https://imaginedragons.fandom.com/wiki/Imagine_Dragons,
https://imaginedragons.fandom.com/wiki/Dave_Lemke
"Imagine Dragons Interview With Guitarist Wayne Sermon | Interview | Music News | JAM Magazine Online | David Dunn | Chris Eason".
jammagazine.com. Archived from the original on 2014-07-15. Retrieved 2014-07-13
https://web.archive.org/web/20141216012750/,
http://www.fasterlouder.com.au/features/36345/Imagine-Dragons-That-arena-sound-excites-us-we-dont-need-to-apologise-for-it
https://web.archive.org/web/20140715001620/,
http://jammagazine.com/mf201302-imagine-dragons-its-time-interview-guitarist-wayne-sermon-writer-david-dunn.aspx#,
Source: Reddit
https://www.youtube.com/watch?v=VQmBx_ZYd5Q
Plenke, Max (November 17, 2011). "Imagine Dragons scores major-label deal".
Las Vegas CityLife. Archived from the original on April 25, 2012. Retrieved July 23, 2015.,
https://web.archive.org/web/20160304100830/,
http://vegasseven.com/2011/11/17/vegas-band-imagine-dragons-sign-interscope/
https://www.youtube.com/watch?v=VQmBx_ZYd5Q
https://www.youtube.com/watch?v=wwpxxIwupgk
https://www.discogs.com/artist/2727700-Imagine-Dragons
https://www.allmusic.com/artist/imagine-dragons-mn0002040645/biography
https://www.reddit.com/r/IAmA/comments/25hxo7/iama_ryan_walker_touring_member_of_imagine/
https://www.discogs.com/artist/2727700-Imagine-Dragons,
https://www.reddit.com/r/imaginedragons/comments/gcacn9/cover_artwork_for_nightvisions/Imagine Dragons interview - Dan and Wayne,
https://www.imaginedragonsmusic.com
https://atwoodmagazine.com/smoke-and-mirrors-conversation-imagine-dragons/https://web.archive.org/web/20140102194744/
http://roccosphere.tumblr.com/post/30933217936/new-imagine-dragons-night-visions-is-5-this-week ,
https://imaginedragons.fandom.com/wiki/Night_Visions
https://www.youtube.com/watch?v=YRfc3j0QjgQ
https://www.youtube.com/watch?v=sENM2wA_FTg,
https://www.youtube.com/watch?v=w5tWYmIOWGk
https://www.youtube.com/watch?v=QrTUUIRZotQ
https://www.youtube.com/watch?v=YRfc3j0QjgQ
https://www.youtube.com/watch?v=ktvTqknDobU,
https://www.youtube.com/watch?v=mWRsgZuwf_8
https://www.youtube.com/watch?v=ktvTqknDobU
https://www.youtube.com/watch?v=mWRsgZuwf_8
http://b-sides.tv/news/20120604-awolnation-announce-tour-with-imagine-dragons
https://seatgeek.com/tba/music/imagine-dragons-arena-tour-dates-concert-tickets/
Ryan Walkers Instagram Account
https://diffuser.fm/imagine-dragons-2012-tour-dates/
https://www.youtube.com/watch?v=vHJyQGnkbDw
https://www.reddit.com/r/imaginedragons/comments/m9vun1/the story of how its time initially had parts of/
https://genius.com/Imagine-dragons-lost-cause-lyrics
https://www.last.fm/music/Imagine+Dragons/The+Archive
https://www.songkick.com/concerts/13605439-imagine-dragons-at-independent-records
https://www.youtube.com/watch?v=7NKAXboKONE&list=PLLaxTiydXayCPMNOnEa2nyR9T4Jv9qaEZ
https://genius.com/Imagine-dragons-ready-aim-fire-lyrics
https://music.apple.com/us/album/itunes-session-ep/1440819698
:https://www.last.fm/music/Imagine+Dragons/Night+Visions+Live
https://www.discogs.com/Imagine-Dragons-Live-At-Lowlands/release/6669267
https://www.imaginedragonsmusic.com/protected-node?destination=node/13236&protected_page=13236
https://www.last.fm/music/Imagine+Dragons/_/Battle+Cry

https://www.youtube.com/watch?v=iBK9GTKArKg
https://www.imaginedragonsmusic.com
https://www.setlist.fm/setlist/imagine-dragons/2015/margaret-court-arena-melbourne-australia-5bf707c8.html
https://www.youtube.com/watch?v=JyictFNpwM8
https://www.imaginedragonsmusic.com
https://en.wikipedia.org/wiki/Smoke_%2B_Mirrors
https://vegas.eater.com/2015/2/13/8037187/imagine-dragons-take-over-the-hard-rock-cafe-on-the-strip
https://en.wikipedia.org/wiki/Smoke_+_Mirrors#cite_note-vegasseven.com-29
http://vegasseven.com/2015/01/29/imagine-dragons-sophomore-album-just-smoke-mirrors/
https://www.howold.co/person/tim-cantor/biography
https://mashable.com/2015/02/09/imagine-dragons-target-live-commercial-ad/
https://www.reviewjournal.com/entertainment/teen-finds-imagine-dragons-treasure-hidden-in-vegas-desert/
http://destinationdragons.com
https://la.curbed.com/2015/10/2/9915172/cliftons-delay-imagine-dragons
https://www.discogs.com/Imagine-Dragons-Smoke-Mirrors-Live/release/16091518
https://www.billboard.com/music/imagine-dragons/chart-history/ARK/2
https://www.youtube.com/watch?v=1gnligd6pBQ
https://www.discogs.com/Imagine-Dragons-Smoke-Mirrors-Live/release/16091518
https://www.youtube.com/watch?v=iBK9GTKArKg
https://www.timcantor.com/tim-cantor-main-menu.html
Chat with Tim Cantor and his wife Amy on Facebook July 2021
https://www.youtube.com/watch?v=4ht80uzIhNs
https://www.billboard.com/articles/news/6406366/imagine-dragons-gold-smoke-mirrors-artwork-premiere
According to a post of Daniel Platzman in February 2015
https://www.youtube.com/watch?v=Rl3ELiPXFRo
https://atwoodmagazine.com/imagine-dragons-album-preview-darkness-shots/
https://www.youtube.com/watch?v=qQrgto184Tk
https://www.idolator.com/7611263/imagine-dragons-united-nations-sap-i-was-me-charity-single?safari=1
https://www.youtube.com/watch?v=USt_qzvuI88
https://en.wikipedia.org/wiki/Smoke_%2B_Mirrors
https://en.wikipedia.org/wiki/Imagine_Dragons_discography
https://www.spotify.com/at/
https://socurrent.com/imagine-dragons-meet-orange-is-the-new-black/
https://www.reddit.com/r/imaginedragons/comments/qr5g9q/were_imagine_dragons_and_were_neither_a/
https://www.youtube.com/watch?v=yI3v6KfR9Mw
https://www.youtube.com/watch?v=GdjRlJ3xii4
https://www.youtube.com/watch?v=F1Vgu237AbU
https://www.riaa.com/gold-platinum/?tab_active=default-
award&ar=Imagine+Dragons&ti=Warriors&format=Single&type=#search_section
https://www.youtube.com/watch?v=9PSysSxRRys
https://www.youtube.com/watch?v=VSB4wGIdDwo
https://en.wikipedia.org/wiki/Evolve_(Imagine_Dragons_album)
https://genius.com/X-ambassadors-fear-lyrics
https://en.wikipedia.org/wiki/Evolve_(Imagine_Dragons_album)
https://blog.terravirtua.io/art/an-interview-with-world-famous-fine-artist-tim-cantor-as-he-breaks-into-the-digital-art-space-
creating-his-very-first-nfts/
https://twitter.com/Imaginedragons
https://www.reddit.com/r/Music/comments/6jm776/this_is_imagine_dragons_our_new_album_evolve_is/
https://create.adobe.com/2017/3/14/matt_eastin_jumps_in_with_both_feet.html
Matt Eastin´s Facebook page
https://www.allmusic.com/album/release/whatever-it-takes-mr0004719034
https://www.imaginedragonsmusic.com/videos/imagine-dragons-evolve-album-art-fan-surprise-pt-1
https://dailytrojan.com/2017/06/20/imagine-dragons-bring-hits-life-virtual-reality-concert/
https://twitter.com/Imaginedragons/status/875392292269338624
http://abcnewsradioonline.com/music-news/2015/9/30/dan-reynolds-looks-back-at-his-childhood-in-imagine-dragons.html
Matt Eastin FB page
https://www.youtube.com/watch?v=7wtfhZwyrcc
https://ew.com/music/2017/03/07/imagine-dragons-dolph-lundgren-believer-video/
https://www.nbcwashington.com/news/national-international/man-who-won-imagine-dragons-music-video-editing-contest/2052479
https://www.youtube.com/watch?v=fKopy74weus
https://www.youtube.com/watch?v=AHDAHCONqp8
https://www.youtube.com/watch?v=I2e_r81Updw
https://www.youtube.com/watch?v=gOsM-DYAEhY
https://www.altpress.com/features/accomplished_music_video_creator_matt_eastin_gives_invaluable_advice_to_asp/
https://www.youtube.com/watch?v=gOsM-DYAEhY
https://creativecloud.adobe.com/de/discover/article/matt-eastin-jumps-in-with-both-feet
Private Information Interview Instagram June 13rd 2021 with Mr. Eastin
http://matteastin.squarespace.com
https://vimeo.com/21349434
https://www.billboard.com/articles/news/vmas/8471097/vma-2018-winners/
https://www.youtube.com/watch?v=qEcOSJXUjVQ
https://www.youtube.com/watch?v=Txlk7PiHaGk
https://www.ableton.com/en/blog/imagine-dragons-from-home-studio-to-shangri-la/
https://www.songfacts.com/facts/imagine-dragons/next-to-me
https://www.billboard.com/articles/columns/rock/8239703/imagine-dragons-next-to-me-video-mini-movie
https://create.adobe.com/2017/3/14/matt_eastin_jumps_in_with_both_feet.html
https://create.adobe.com/2017/3/14/matt_eastin_jumps_in_with_both_feet.html
https://www.youtube.com/watch?v=PscXGpsF3dY
https://themilsource.com/2021/03/22/who-is-beeple-aka-mike-winkelmann/
https://www.beeple-crap.com
https://www.theverge.com/2020/1/3/21046790/beeple-mike-winkelmann-interview-everyday-post-apocalyptic-baby-yoda-
zuckerberg
https://motionographer.com/2015/09/23/zero-day-process-and-qa/
https://www.esquire.com/entertainment/a35500985/who-is-beeple-mike-winkelmann-nft-interview/
https://guttulus.com/beeple-mike-winkelmann-the-most-famous-nft-artist-20-facts/
https://www.castellodirivoli.org/en/mike-winkelmann-beeple/
https://twitter.com/Imaginedragons/status/861975951688687621
https://www.last.fm/music/Imagine+Dragons/Live+At+AllSaints+Studios
https://shop.imaginedragonsmusic.com/collections/music-1/products/imagine-dragons-limited-edition-vinyl-box-set
https://www.discogs.com/Imagine-Dragons-Night-Visions-Smoke-Mirrors-Evolve/release/13710720
https://www.discogs.com/Imagine-Dragons-German-Radio-Live-Sessions/release/12798476
https://www.nme.com/news/music/imagine-dragons-reveal-release-date-new-album-origins-2386760

https://en.wikipedia.org/wiki/Origins_(Imagine_Dragons_album)
https://www.youtube.com/watch?v=NapLxHp09DU
https://www.spotify.com/at/
https://www.iheart.com/content/2018-07-17-imagine-dragons-share-new-song-natural-espns-college-football-anthem/
https://www.reddit.com/r/imaginedragons/comments/9wg6j8/effort_opinion_and_long_post_i_solved_origins_and/
https://www.youtube.com/watch?v=5kwn3YUZArY
Radio station New Music daily with MAJAN, Interview with Dan on July 1st 2021
https://mythopedia.com/roman-mythology/gods/mercury/
https://www.britannica.com/biography/Rick-Rubin
https://m.youtube.com/watch?v=D77edwNcFT8&feature=youtu.be
https://www.youtube.com/watch?v=hHb4ynObZWO
https://www.youtube.com/watch?v=m8tJDg3weNU
https://www.youtube.com/watch?v=EjdsBfKsLJY
https://www.iheart.com/content/2021-05-12-watch-imagine-dragons-perform-follow-you-with-a-classroom-full-of-kids/
https://wtmx.com/imagine-dragons-launches-follow-you-video-game-new-speedrun-video/
Imagine Dragons´ Twitter Account
https://www.youtube.com/watch?v=hUyx3O7INyI
https://www.youtube.com/watch?v=01w2oQGxBqI
https://www.youtube.com/watch?v=jfkW9J8_oDw
https://www.youtube.com/watch?v=hUyx3O7INyI (Interview with Rachel Smith)
https://www.youtube.com/watch?v=01w2oQGxBqI
Matt Eastin´s Facebook page
Dan Reynolds TikTok Account, Dan Reynolds Twitter Account
According to a post on Instagram by user @latviab. She commented that on Matt Eastin contribution for the Wrecked MV on July 16th 2021
Live Chat with Dan right before the music video release of Wrecked on Youtube July, 15th, 2021
Thank you note at the YouTube page of the official Music Video to Wrecked
Live Chat with Dan right before the music video release of Wrecked on Youtube July, 15th, 2021
https://wfpk.org/2021/imagine-dragons-this-new-record-thematically-dives-into-the-finality-of-life/
https://eu.usatoday.com/story/entertainment/music/2021/09/02/imagine-dragons-dan-reynolds-talks-vulnerable-songs-new-album-reconciled-wife-lgbtq-acceptance/5668679001
https://bigactive.com/music-art-direction-design/music/imagine-dragons/
https://www.youtube.com/watch?v=CQ39byE7OOU
https://www.youtube.com/watch?v=5RoQ86nyfaQ
https://www.youtube.com/watch?v=t42EqwM3CZU
https://eu.usatoday.com/story/entertainment/music/2021/09/02/imagine-dragons-dan-reynolds-talks-vulnerable-songs-new-album-reconciled-wife-lgbtq-acceptance/5668679001/
https://wfpk.org/2021/imagine-dragons-this-new-record-thematically-dives-into-the-finality-of-life/
Live Chat with Dan right before the music video release of Wrecked on Youtube July, 15th, 2021
https://www.imaginedragonsmusic.com/tour
https://www.youtube.com/watch?v=N8H-vtdO-DQ
https://www.linkedin.com/company/polymathvisuals
Instagram post of Andrew Tolman from Sept. 3, 2021
https://www.ableton.com/en/blog/imagine-dragons-from-home-studio-to-shangri-la/
https://finance.yahoo.com/news/imagine-dragons-reveal-demons-telykast-130000001.html?guccounter=1&guce_referrer=aHR0cHM6Ly9kdWNrZHVja2dvLmNvbS8&guce_referrer_sig=AQAAACp-L97Kgz3U3HdcnaS1c3AlTth-08c4KCY4Mge_1QteswDh8ObclJzqYhj7_U
https://www.reddit.com/r/imaginedragons/comments/qr5g9q/were_imagine_dragons_and_were_neither_a/
https://techstory.in/league-of-legends-gets-a-new-music-video-for-arcane-featuring-imagine-dragons/
https://www.laut.de/Rick-Rubin
https://www.loudersound.com/features/rick-rubin-a-guide-to-his-best-albums
https://www.sho.com/shangri-la
https://www.loudersound.com/features/rick-rubin-a-guide-to-his-best-albums
https://www.britannica.com/biography/Rick-Rubin
https://www.grammy.com/grammys/artists/rick-rubin/13812
https://www.thefader.com/2015/09/28/rick-rubin-interview
https://ew.com/article/1993/09/10/rick-rubins-labels-name-change/
https://www.imdb.com/name/nm0005391/bio
https://www.latimes.com/archives/la-xpm-2007-feb-11-ca-rubin11-story.html
https://sport.sky.it/calcio/europa-league/2022/03/16/europa-league-conference-league-su-sky-imagine-dragons-video
https://www.target.com/p/imagine-dragons-mercury-8211-acts-1-38-2-target-exclusive-cd/-/A-86435342
https://themusicuniverse.com/imagine-dragons-releasing-mercury-double-album/?fbclid=IwAR1E8SOlPVWEJ1Ck24zhieaF-ZKiVwQVUjtlp3ryduZZ-mKQJY9yRS6QD64
Mac Reynold´s LinkedIn Account
https://fluence.io/macreynolds
https://fatheringexcellence.com/episodes/ep-6-father-of-dan-reynolds-imagine-dragons-singer-ron-reynolds
http://reynoldslawyers.com/MatthewReynolds/
https://www.linkedin.com/in/dalyn-bauman-30850674/
https://www.tvbeurope.com/tveverywhere/imagine-dragons-use-telestream-wirecast-stream-live-twitch
Turner Pope´s LinkedIn account
https://americansongwriter.com/songwriter-u-qa-alex-da-kid-discovering-imagine-dragons-crafting-tracks-rihanna-eminem-u2/
https://isittoolatenow.blogspot.com/2007/08/corey-fox.html
https://utahvalley360.com/2017/06/26/velour-owner-celebrates-life-after-receiving-kidney-transplant-local-musician/
https://www.youtube.com/watch?v=t42EqwM3CZU
https://people.com/music/imagine-dragons-to-throw-benefit-livestream-to-save-concert-venue/
https://www.slugmag.com/music/interviews/music-interviews/velour-live-music-gallery-a-home-a-church-and-a-venue/
Imagine Dragons Twitter Account, iHeart Radio album release party (Mercury Act 1) and ID´s performance in London at the Pryzm in November 2021
https://fohonline.com/articles/production-profile/imagine-dragons-mercury-tour/
Various ID live performances, for example their concert in Paris, Lollapalooza 2018.
https://fohonline.com/articles/production-profile/imagine-dragons-mercury-tour/
Angie Warner´s Instagram Account
https://www.psu.edu/news/impact/story/love-music-powers-bellisario-college-alumnus-career/
https://www.linkedin.com/in/james-jt-taylor-7422a034/
https://fohonline.com/articles/production-profile/imagine-dragons-mercury-tour/
Corey Fox Facebook account March, 14th 2012
https://www.imdb.com/name/nm3638923/bio?ref_=nm_ov_bio_sm
http://www.isaachalasima.com/#//imagine-dragons-smoke-and-mirrors/
https://www.youtube.com/watch?v=CdWd8fUC71g
https://www.youtube.com/watch?v=Mq4m3yAoW8E
https://247sports.com/Article/ESPN-picks-pump-up-song-for-the-2018-college-football-season-119870184/

https://eu.usatoday.com/story/life/entertainthis/2018/01/29/marijuana-trucks-japanese-toilet-celebs-divulge-their-first-big-paycheck-splurges/1074987001/https://www.youtube.com/watch?v=OI647GU3Jsc
https://www.billboard.com/articles/news/8475986/imagine-dragons-zero-video
https://www.youtube.com/watch?v=PSAPGjnaKCA
https://www.youtube.com/watch?v=j60ClcNYWu4
https://m.youtube.com/watch?v=LObzpbvysds
https://www.youtube.com/watch?v=I-QfPUz1es8
https://www.youtube.com/watch?v=vOXZkm9p_zY
https://www.youtube.com/watch?v=_G-k6TQYUek
https://www.youtube.com/watch?v=1DoI5WTjd3w
https://www.spotify.com/at
https://www.washingtontimes.com/news/2016/may/10/x-ambassadors-singer-sam-harris-how-imagine-dragon/
https://www.youtube.com/watch?v=YRfc3j0QjgQ
https://genius.com/Lil-wayne-wiz-khalifa-imagine-dragons-logic-and-ty-dolla-sign-sucker-for-pain-lyrics
https://www.songmeaningsandfacts.com/meaning-of-radioactive-by-imagine-dragons/
https://twitter.com/pandoramusic/status/1062807387717783552
https://genius.com/Avicii-and-imagine-dragons-heart-upon-my-sleeve-lyrics
https://www.passiton.com/inspirational-stories-tv-spots/166-love
https://twitter.com (Imagine Dragons Account, Oct, 20th, 2018
https://www.redbull.com/us-en/imagine-dragons-interview
https://www.youtube.com/watch?v=t42EqwM3CZU
https://www.discogs.com/Imagine-Dragons-Night-Visions-Smoke-Mirrors-Evolve-Origins/release/14506776
https://www.discogs.com/Imagine-Dragons-Radioactive-Demons-Thunder-Bad-Liar/release/16031972
https://www.imaginedragonsmusic.com
https://bold.org/scholarships/imagine-dragons-scholarship/
https://famousmormons.net/mormon-entertainment/famous-mormon-musicians/imagine-dragons/
https://www.youtube.com/watch?v=tEgZWA1avVA
https://www.youtube.com/watch?v=Q7-yRMwopE0
https://www.goldenplec.com/imagine-dragons-interview/
Posted on Reddit on July, 24th 2021 by a user called DeSpencerDiSpenser.
https://celebanswers.com/what-was-imagine-dragons-first-song/
https://web.archive.org/web/20150722094512/
http://www.drummagazine.com/features/post/daniel-platzman-dream-the-wildest-dreams/P2/
https://www.billboard.com/articles/events/bbma-2014/6092007/imagine-dragons-talk-second-album-radioactive-success-at-billboard-music-awards
Twitter - @gingerika fan account
https://www.reddit.com/r/imaginedragons/comments/qr5g9q/were_imagine_dragons_and_were_neither_a/
https://www.youtube.com/watch?v=wwpxxIwupgk
https://www.today.com/health/rock-singer-undergoes-kidney-transplant-surgery-save-his-mentor-s-t114378
https://www.youtube.com/watch?v=BpA4wHXi1-w
https://www.drummersresource.com/daniel-platzman-imagine-dragons-interview/
https://www.thenationalnews.com/business/money/2022/04/04/generation-start-up-how-imagine-dragons-inspired-egypts-first-digital-trading-app/
https://ew.com/article/2013/03/29/year-dragons/
https://www.youtube.com/watch?v=R3_htbh_Jdw
https://www.youtube.com/watch?v=26BsqkILiwU
https://www.udiscovermusic.com/stories/smoke-and-mirrors-imagine-dragons-album/
https://www.grammy.com/grammys/artists/imagine-dragons/18215
https://vgost.fandom.com/wiki/Imagine_Dragons
https://www.youtube.com/watch?v=R3_htbh_Jdw
https://www.youtube.com/watch?v=qWMrOeARr24
https://www.youtube.com/watch?v=RJ2b2UuYObY
https://www.grammy.com/grammys/artists/imagine-dragons/18215
https://archive.is/20130127092444/
http://www.lasvegascitylife.com/articles/2009/07/06/music/fear_and_lounging/iq_29705856.txt
https://ksltv.com/492781/imagine-dragons-zions-bank-surprise-velour-owner-with-paid-off-mortgage/
iHeart Radio Canada Interview, March, 24th, 2021
https://atwoodmagazine.com/smoke-and-mirrors-conversation-imagine-dragons/
https://www.youtube.com/watch?v=4-glU8ns6us
https://podcasts.apple.com/at/podcast/001-dan-reynolds-imagine-dragons/id1405795796?i=1000415451286
https://metro.co.uk/2013/02/05/dan-reynolds-its-time-is-a-song-i-wrote-at-a-low-point-in-my-life-3380799/
Dan Reynolds (Imagine Dragons) - Ice Bucked Challenge - 19.08.2014 Stadtpark Hamburg
https://podcasts.apple.com/at/podcast/001-dan-reynolds-imagine-dragons/id1405795796?i=1000415451286
https://www.youtube.com/watch?v=Y-kwuLNBPQs
https://genius.com/Imagine-dragons-stars-lyrics
https://create.adobe.com/2017/3/14/matt_eastin_jumps_in_with_both_feet.html
https://www.youtube.com/watch?v=wwpxxIwupgk
https://www.last.fm/music/Imagine+Dragons/_/Speak+to+Me
http://www.fasterlouder.com.au/features/36345/Imagine-Dragons-That-arena-sound-excites-us-we-dont-need-to-apologise-for-it#7oszDfaxPluAwUX6.99
https://www.youtube.com/watch?v=YhhbD2d1mxA
https://latterdaysaintmusicians.com/artists/imagine-dragons
https://musichistorian.net/2012/03/26/opening-doors-imagine-dragons-bassist-ben-mckee-talks-about-the-bands-exciting-journey/
https://www.setlist.fm/search?artist=5bd1b7fc&query=tour:%28Imagine+Dragons+on+Tour%29
https://vegasmagazine.com/digital-editions 2015 issue 1 spring
https://musichistorian.net/2012/03/26/opening-doors-imagine-dragons-bassist-ben-mckee-talks-about-the-bands-exciting-journey/
https://www.riaa.com/gold-platinum/?tab_active=default-award&se=imagine+dragons#search_section
https://www.kulturecity.org/kultureball-2021/
Dan Reynolds Twitter Account Nov 10th 2021
https://college.berklee.edu/news/students-backstage-with-imagine-dragons
https://www.youtube.com/watch?v=EijklbgZQcg
https://www.youtube.com/watch?v=xqkKNR__EyY
https://www.youtube.com/watch?v=TZs4F3-GsN8
https://www.bmi.com/news/entry/imagine_dragons_a_good_bet
https://m.youtube.com/watch?v=olT3MZa5GsA
https://lasvegassun.com/news/2010/mar/17/wrapping-reverb/
https://www.youtube.com/watch?v=YTQe7w1wGjY
https://www.heraldextra.com/entertainment/music/fork-fest-revival-unites-utah-music-scene-with-3-stages-28-bands/article_c3ca4f3e-bf8e-5857-aa83-5a7e7bf91e12.html
https://www.worthpoint.com/worthopedia/one-kind-imagine-dragons-cd-self-1832849993
https://rateyourmusic.com/release/ep/imagine-dragons/its-time/
https://issuu.com/search?q=imagine%20dragons

https://www.festivalticker.de/2011/festivals/bergenfest/
https://imaginedragons.fandom.com/wiki/Andrew_Tolman
https://imaginedragons.fandom.com/wiki/Theresa_Flaminio
https://lasvegasweekly.com/news/2011/jul/29/imagine-dragons-get-new-look-and-make-lots-new-pla/
http://www.fasterlouder.com.au/features/36345/Imagine-Dragons-That-arena-sound-excites-us-we-dont-need-to-apologise-for-it#7oszDfaxPluAwUX6.99
https://www.youtube.com/watch?v=UXvZTwJ4vho
https://www.youtube.com/watch?v=YRfc3j0QjgQ
https://www.youtube.com/watch?v=VQmBx_ZYd5Q
https://www.liveabout.com/imagine-dragons-profile-4149815
https://imaginedragons.fandom.com/wiki/Theresa_Flaminio
https://video.search.yahoo.com/search/
video;_ylt=AwrJ7J1nJLifO10AV9NXNyoA;_ylu=Y29sbwNiZjEEcG9zAzMEdnRpANBMDYxNV8xBHNlYwNzYw--?
p=music+video+2012+best&fr=uh_magentertain_web_gs
https://www.youtube.com/watch?v=_ZczEMPcnsY
https://www.youtube.com/watch?v=xTunmZD3qHY
https://www.idolator.com/7235392/imagine-dragons-late-night-fallon-video?safari=1
https://en.wikipedia.org/wiki/Night_Visions
http://b-sides.tv/news/20120604-awolnation-announce-tour-with-imagine-dragons
https://www.glastonburyfestivals.co.uk/line-up/line-up-2014
https://en.wikipedia.org/wiki/Night_Visions
https://www.facebook.com/?locale=de_DE
https://www.amfm-magazine.com/imagine-dragons-film-the-making-of-night-visions/
https://www.youtube.com/watch?v=WaZzNv_SOwA
https://www.youtube.com/watch?v=eDjVvOmpE4s
https://www.grammy.com/grammys/artists/imagine-dragons/18215
https://web.archive.org/web/20150722094512/
http://www.drummagazine.com/features/post/daniel-platzman-dream-the-wildest-dreams/P2/
https://en.wikipedia.org/wiki/Glastonbury_Festival#Location
https://www.youtube.com/watch?v=oqYoDC2RVCg
https://www.youtube.com/watch?v=QZATTFyZfsc
https://www.imdb.com/name/nm4995251/?ref_=fn_al_nm_1
https://www.billboard.com/articles/news/6164956/weird-al-yankovic-inactive-imagine-dragons-response
https://www.trf.org/trf-gala-2014/
https://m.imdb.com/name/nm4995251/trivia?ref_=m_nm_dyk_trv
https://en.wikipedia.org/wiki/Smoke_%2B_Mirrors
https://m.imdb.com/name/nm4995251/trivia?ref_=m_nm_dyk_trv
https://www.youtube.com/watch?v=HnCTvVjdh8k
https://genius.com/Imagine-dragons-wings-lyrics#about
https://lasvegassun.com/blogs/kats-report/2016/jul/25/imagine-dragons-dan-reynolds-joins-the-parody-prot/
https://www.youtube.com/watch?v=hoPqRZaxxyI
https://www.ktnv.com/news/imagine-dragons-the-killers-to-headline-vegas-strong-benefit-concert
https://www.musicbusinessworldwide.com/concord-music-publishing-acquires-imagine-dragons-catalog-in-100m-deal
https://www.adweek.com/digital/live-nation-livestream-imagine-dragons-twitter/
https://eatsleepedm.com/kygo-reveals-born-to-be-yours-with-imagine-dragons/
https://www.corning.com/gorillaglass/worldwide/en/origins.html
https://www.pocketgamer.com/articles/078594/angry-birds-and-imagine-dragons-come-together-in-a-charming-collaboration/
https://venturebeat.com/2019/06/10/beat-saber-gets-10-imagine-dragons-song-pack-and-a-new-360-degree-vr-level/
https://www.uefa.com/insideuefa/about-uefa/news/0251-0f8e6b5a0723-f67054204b9e-1000--imagine-dragons-to-perform-at-2019-uefa-champions-league-final-/
https://www.nme.com/features/gaming-features/imagine-dragons-on-their-collaborations-with-kindred-spirits-riot-games-3097505
https://gamingeek77.com/tsm-bjergsen-coaches-daniel-platzman-from-imagine-dragons
https://www.tvbeurope.com/tvbeverywhere/imagine-dragons-use-telestream-wirecast-stream-live-twitc
https://www.youtube.com/watch?v=THt75X5pDnI
https://www.youtube.com/watch?v=tOJYymcVmVE
https://clios.com/music/winner/partnerships-collaborations/arcane-league-of-legends/imagine-dragons-enemy-with-jid-from-the-series-arc-117185
Live Interview on Apple Music with Hanuman Welch June 26th 2022
https://www.looktothestars.org/video/1270-hands-a-song-for-orlando
http://www.toyotagiving.com
https://www.musiciansoncall.org/what-we-do/
https://www.kulturecity.org
https://vm.tiktok.com/ZMRyMcbwv/
https://deluxe-version.com/slaying-cancer-with-imagine-dragons-at-the-rise-up-trf-gala/
https://edition.cnn.com/2019/12/16/entertainment/imagine-dragons-dan-reynolds/index.html
https://open.spotify.com/artist/53XhwfbYqKCa1cC15pYq2q
https://genius.com/Imagine-dragons-wings-lyrics#about
https://www.trf.org/gala2020/
https://fandiem.com/sweeps/imaginedragons-spain
https://www.billboard.com/articles/columns/rock/6620412/imagine-dragons-radioactive-riaa-certified-diamond
https://open.spotify.com/artist/53XhwfbYqKCa1cC15pYq2q
http://blbrd.cm/FsyP56j
https://www.imaginedragonsmusic.com
https://california18.com/nrj-music-awards-2021-the-winners-of-the-evening/1619332021/
https://www.youtube.com/watch?v=mStJDg3weNU
https://www.youtube.com/watch?v=EjdsBfKsLJY
https://www.iheart.com/content/2021-05-18-imagine-dragons-dan-reynolds-shows-gratitude-for-believer-going-diamond/
https://www.youtube.com/watch?v=aCqv-X7a8NA
Cellphone App TikTok
FaceTime Interview with Jesse Robinson May 2nd 2022
https://www.youtube.com/watch?v=Wbm9gDPRVcM
https://www.youtube.com/watch?v=ujuBjMOaDdM
https://www.youtube.com/watch?v=YO-OCzdxhO0
https://www.youtube.com/watch?v=O6j1uFt4tCw
https://www.youtube.com/watch?v=6x9CAAqzG24
https://www.youtube.com/watch?v=jfKLcPLxXSg
https://www.youtube.com/watch?v=5CF60icPR90
https://www.youtube.com/watch?v=ckOqqHmIG-c
https://www.youtube.com/watch?v=LPR8GoJDEaA
https://www.youtube.com/watch?v=UJW3afTKVOo
https://www.youtube.com/watch?v=G3JGH1sNYUY
https://www.youtube.com/watch?v=kqQi5NiEufw

https://www.youtube.com/watch?v=tOJYymcVmVE
https://www.youtube.com/watch?v=3t1ONLAJ_Rs
https://www.aceshowbiz.com/celebrity/imagine_dragons/awards.html
https://www.trf.org
Interview with executive director Kim Gradisher from May 27th, 2021
https://www.artistdirect.com/imagine-dragons/news/imagine-dragons-and-trf-team-with-hard-rock-for-charity-shirt-and-pin/111283
https://www.prnewswire.com/news-releases/stage-rush-imagine-dragons-helps-families-fighting-childhood-cancer-300215926.html
https://footwearnews.com/2018/shop/sneakers-deals/imagine-dragons-superga-zappos-sneaker-release-info-1202690879/
https://www.angrybirds.com/blog/imagine-dragons-rock-good-cause-angry-birds-match/
http://www.casinocitytimes.com/news/article/new-years-eve-with-imagine-dragons-228383
https://imaginedragonsdaily.tumblr.com/post/166330884772/spoiler-alert-whatever-it-takes-mystery-solved
executive Interview with Matt Eastin on Instagram
https://www.omaze.com/products/imagine-dragons-zero-gravity
https://www.dtwt.org/imaginedragons/imagine-dragons
https://blog.amnestyusa.org/music-and-the-arts/why-amnestyinternationalusa-is-wishing-imagine-dragons-good-luck-at-the-grammys/
https://www.reviewjournal.com/entertainment/music/imagine-dragons-gives-surprise-performance-in-front-of-bellagio/
https://www.idolator.com/7611263/imagine-dragons-united-nations-sap-i-was-me-charity-single?safari=1&Exc_TM_LessThanPoint001_p1=1
https://medium.com/cuepoint/imagine-dragons-cares-about-the-refugee-crisis-and-you-should-too-26e5620d07cf#.2qqf4hwcu
https://m.imdb.com/name/nm4995251/trivia?ref_=m_nm_dyk_trv
Song lyric taken from Booklets (Night Visions, Smoke + Mirrors
https://genius.com/Imagine-dragons-wrecked-lyrics
https://en.everybodywiki.com/Jorgen_Odegard
https://twitter.com
https://www.facebook.com
Apple Maps
Opinions from Twitter users from Imagine Dragons fandom
Imagine Dragons Instagram posts

We hope, you enjoyed this book...

Name: Kenny

Nationality: Greek

Things, I love: music, movies, photography, sunsets/sunrises, nature, Imagine Dragons, traveling

Things I dislike: lies, injustice, hypocrisy, two-faced and snobbish people dishonesty and bullying

I´m a fan of Imagine Dragons because:

They are the best, not only as a band but as people and that's based on their actions towards their fans and the whole world, in general. Down-to earth above all.

Name: Ingrid

Nationality: Austrian

Things I love: I enjoy it to travel and to discover foreign cultures, I love to cook dishes from all over the world, Imagine Dragons and to chat for hours with friends

Things I dislike: intolerance, prejudice, dishonesty, injustice, arrogant and homophobic people

I´m a fan of Imagine Dragons because:

Their lyrics and songs touch my heart and soul and it´s obvious, they care a lot about humans by their beneficence. That's another thing I love about them. It's just a full package...

Name: Anastasia

Nationality: Russian

The artwork for this book was done by me. From childhood, art has always been a passion of mine and now its grown from a hobby, to my life. It is my everything, I find inspiration in all that surrounds me, including Imagine Dragons whose music and attitude to life have been a huge influence.

To see more of my work, please visit my Instagram accounts:
anastasiablinkova_
a.blinkova_

Name: Rachel
Nationality: American

I wrote the poetry featured in this book. Writing has been my passion since I was young, and through my books and poetry, I love exploring themes of humanity and our shared emotional experiences. Imagine Dragons mean a lot to me because of the way they use those same themes—it feels real and raw, and it inspires me in my own creations.

Name: Celeste
Nationality: Canadian

Hi, I´m Celeste and I did the editing for part 2.0 of this book. Despite not being a professional editor, I jumped at the chance to be able to do this when I was asked to help, because I saw it is a way for me to help The Tyler Robinson Foundation and in doing so, thank Imagine Dragons. Words can't explain the gratitude I feel for ID. Their music and words have given me hope in bad times and been a consistent light in my life. Tyler Robinson has inspired me with his story, seeing the strength and positivity that he had, despite the hardship he faced. I am so very glad that by taking part in this book that I can play a small part in helping other families who are facing the same adversity.

Live in regret, or eye to the future?
I'd rather be here,
Thinking about the now
´Cause this breath could fade fast
And this day could be your last

Waves
Mercury Act 1 & 2

Printed in Great Britain
by Amazon